FROM A BOY TO A MAN

McArthur Billing

Order this book online at www.trafford.com
or email orders@trafford.com

Most Trafford titles are also available at major online book retailers.

Note for Librarians: A cataloguing record for this book is available from Library
and Archives Canada at www.collectionscanada.ca/amicus/index-e.html

Printed in Victoria, BC, Canada.

ISBN: 978-1-4269-0472-1 (sc)

*Our mission is to efficiently provide the world's finest, most comprehensive book publishing
service, enabling every author to experience success. To find out how to publish your
book, your way, and have it available worldwide, visit us online at www.trafford.com*

Trafford rev. 9/2/2009

 www.trafford.com

North America & international
toll-free: 1 888 232 4444 (USA & Canada)
phone: 250 383 6864 ♦ fax: 812 355 4082

FORWARD

FIRST AND FOREMOST, I would like to thank my wife, Mary, for her support and encouragement as I penned this, my first book. Her constant tugging to try to slow me down made me jump that much harder into high gear to push her to get this book finished.

I would also like to thank my five children, Mark, McArthur, Jr., Gregory, Sandra and Kimberly, my son-in-law, Reginal, and my daughter-in-law Miriam for having belief in my efforts and belief that this project would be a success. To my six grandchildren, Sha, Bethany, Marian, Rachel, Mariah and R. J., who have inspired me more than anyone to write this book. I realize how important it is for them to know the changes that have occurred during my relatively short lifetime.

This book is comprised of experiences I shared growing up in South Arkansas. Many are shared from my home environment, and for that I give credit to a wonderful set of parents, Grady and Elburdie Billing, and my sisters and brothers. I also must remember all the different community people that formed my life and made these stories so interesting.

To my dearest Aunt Rosie Mae McDaniel for her constant support, to my trusted friends Pete and Linda Williams, Linda for typing the first copy of this book. To a very special minister who has been a great inspiration in my life, without him ever knowing it, Rev. D. L. Hegler.

To my co-workers, first there is Marvin Williams. Marvin has been around twenty years. He is gentle, kind and very free-hearted, in fact he will give you the shirt off his back, but he will break your leg if you try to take a penny from him. To Jimmy McKnight, the storyteller, he can tell a story and every story is a very long one. He can tell you about walking in the woods and give such details until you can smell the leaves on the ground. He is really the one that should be writing a book. Then there is Brady Jeffus, he is the type of guy who can be your best friend or he can be your worst enemy; but he's a fair man, he will let you decide which he's going to be. Just don't cross him. Then there's the foreman, John Courtney. He is about as fine a fellow as I every worked around. He's out there on the job and his phi-losophy is, "Let's do it right the first time fellows, we may not have time to do it right the next time around." There is Jason Arnold, he loves hunting and fishing. In fact, if Jason had an opportunity to spend a quite, rainy afternoon at home sitting by a good warm fire with his wife or to go hunting, well, his wife would just have to wait until he gets back from hunting. The only thing Jason likes more than hunting and fishing is more hunting and fishing. Then there's David Hornsby, he has always been a nice guy with whom to work. I remember when David came to the plant shortly after I did, and the only time I heard him talk ugly, was to his lunch bucket. That was the only time I heard David say a bad word. A real nice guy but; he can't wait to retire. He has already bought a motor home and he's just raring to put some miles on the road. Next, there is Stan, he is the newcomer. His philosophy for every job is, "Let's just do this job and get it over with." I've often told him if his father knew what a fine man he'd turned out to be, he would really be proud of him. Then there is Scott Davis and Michael Black. I put these both in the same category because both of them love kids and sports. In fact, both of them coach little league teams and every minute of it they love. Then there is Danny McLemore, he is big and strong. He could go bear hunt-ing with a switch; but you wouldn't find a kinder, gentler or more understanding man to work with than Danny. Last, but not least is Steve Taylor, "My Hero." Steve is a very kind, mild mannered man, easy to get along with, and he will do whatever it takes to keep the peace. He is also a lot of fun to work with; he can put sunshine in anybody's cloudy day.

To my other friends and family whom I didn't have an opportunity to name, thank you all very much for your inspiration in my life.

COUNTRY LIVING

ONE OF THE greatest experiences in the life of a human being is to be born into a loving and caring family. The most phenomenal things about families are we have no choice in the matter, one can choose their friends, but inherits a family. With that being said, I am glad to announce, I was the eighth child of 12 children born to Grady and Elburdie Benton Billing. I was born on a cold, gray day in February, 1941, when life was simple and just to exist was a major effort; but we, the Billing family were on the move in a small farm community comprised of all family members just outside of Strong, Arkansas.

Our community included my grandfather, my mom (his daughter) and dad on our small tract of land, my uncle and his family (my mother's brother) and my aunt and her family (my mother's sister). The rest of the community was all cousins and other relatives.

My father was a row crop farmer and a water well digger. Back in the 1940's almost everyone depended on wells or springs for water. There were no water systems with piped water like we have today. My father's well business consisted of a pickup truck, his pick and shovel and a couple of strong bodies to literally dig and move the dirt. He had a most unique method of locating water. He would use a forked stick. He could walk around a well site and just like a metal detector, when he was over the main vein of water the stick would drop to the ground. He would be unable to stop the stick from dropping every time he came near that spot.

Most of his customers began to rely on this unquestionable gift; my daddy had and would allow him to dig the well at the location of his choice.

We didn't have much of anything of value; we were very poor as were most of our neighbors. Imagine 12 children and a wife with only one man working. We just didn't have much of anything except a determination to survive. Of course all of us were never really home at the same time. The older kids would be up and gone by the time the younger group came along.

My mother was an exceptional woman. She took care of the family, washed, cooked and even raised the garden that fed the family. In fact, we raised everything we ate. There were very few trips to what we today call the grocery store. We lived off the land and the products that it provided. We raised our own cows and they provided milk, butter and meat. To break the ground for the garden we had a horse to plow. My father did not have a tractor. In the spring when my mother would begin to work her garden, we would go into the edge of the woods and rake the leaves and straw back from under the old trees. We would then dig about a 1-1/2 inch of top soil, place it on the slide, which was pulled by the horse and we would put the soil between the rows in the garden. This would give the same effect as new ground. We would pile all of the unwanted material in a corner and let it rot, this was called compost. By using this natural process we did not have to use a commercial fertilizer.

When I was growing up the world was very different from the world of today. We lived in a segregated society. When I went to school it was to a Black school with Black teachers. We lived 2-1/2 miles off the main highway and we had to walk that distance morning and evening to catch the school bus.

But all in all, we had a basically good life. Going to an all Black school still had its ups and downs. We still had class separation. Some families had a little more than others and they never let you forget that. Some families lived in town while others lived out on farms and they were quick to remind you of your *country* status. Indifference doesn't always come with race – indifference comes with just being human.

Although we were of the group that didn't have very much, we never experienced a hungry day in our lives. My mother always made sure we had food and clothing. There was a White family who lived on our road but closer to the main highway, what we called *out front*. They had family who lived in El Dorado and the husband worked at the oil refinery, which was an exceptionally good job. Most of the town people were generous with their resources. They had a habit of giving away clothes they could no longer use. So this family in El Dorado, because of the connection to their country cousins, chose to share their clothing with our family. They donated to our cause. The lady in our community would get the clothes from town and bring them to the country to share with our family. Because of this, we always had plenty of clothes to wear. My mother would accept the clothes, wash, alter, repair, and even re-make until they suited our family's need.

Because we were farmers, it was only natural that we had cows, hogs and chickens. These farm animals were most valuable for meat, milk, butter and eggs. They were our grocery store. They weren't costly to raise either, because we lived so far off the main the road that our animals could run free – open range. They roamed and ate off the land, as we did. Sometimes in the winter when food was scarce, we would give them additional feed to help them make it, but in the summer they lived directly off the land.

Along with the farm animals, we also raised row-crops such as corn, cotton, peas, beans, potatoes, peanuts and sugar cane, which was also used for food – another section of our grocery store, the produce department.

My father would plant 10 – 15 acres of cotton; that was our cash crop. In the fall of the year when the fields were white, and the cotton was ripe and ready to pick, we would begin the gathering process. We would pick the cotton and transport it to the cotton gin, where my father would sell it so we would have money to make it through the winter months.

There was a creek that ran across our property and during the cold winter months my father was a trapper. He would put steal traps along the creek to catch wild game. He would run his traps early in the morning before he went to work and late in the evening after work. The fur bearing animals were skinned and the hides sold to help get money for the family. Again, the meat became a part of our food supply.

In the fall of the year, there was a White man with a cattle truck who would come into our community and buy cows from the families who had cows that were ready to be moved. My father would always sell 2 or 3 cows every fall so we would have a little Christmas money.

Along with going to school, I had to do my farm and house chores. You had to pull your weight in my family. When I was around 12 or 13 years old, a service station was built on the main highway between El Dorado and Strong. Everyday on my way to school we passed by this station and I made a prediction I would work at that station when I got out of school. As I grew older I still had the desire to work at that station. When I finally turned 16, I went to the station and asked for a Saturday job. They gave me a Saturday job. My prediction had come true – I had a job at the station!

FIRST JOB

THE OIL BUSINESS was booming, there were plenty of oil wells in this area. This station also had a shop that serviced lots and lots of trucks and equipment; so there was plenty of work to be done at this place. As time rolled on, they cleared more land out back behind the shop to make room for pipe racks, pulling rigs and all kinds of equipment to be used.

My after school job at the service station consisted of washing and cleaning cars, hauling off trash and just general tasks around the station, I wanted more. I wanted a full-time job; so after I finished high school, I worked for the same people, but in the shop instead of the station.

That's when my life began to change. That's when I had to make some cold hard decisions. Even though I worked in the shop for the boss man, I still washed his car, his wife's car and anybody else's car he told me to wash. There was one other Black guy, a much older guy working at the station. He was working there when I started, but I was the boy out back in the shop and I washed and cleaned oil field trucks.

My washing platform was made of cross ties on the ground, with thick oak boards on them to make a floor wide enough to drive a pickup onto, because if you washed vehicles in the same place for very long, it became a sloppy, muddy mess. So to prevent getting mud in the vehicle from muddy feet, they made the wooden bed to work on and walk.

I was washing a vehicle one day and one of the men that actually worked in the oil field came back and was talking to me. He was really picking at me, or as we would say as kids, "poking fun" at me. We were talking about vehicles and I said "Well I'll have a nice car and a nice house one day." He asked, "What else are you going to have?" I said, "I'm going to build a house with a 2-car garage where I can park my vehicle, probably a pickup truck and my wife's car." He then asked, "And what else are you going to have?" I went on to tell him some other things I was going to have in life. When he stepped back into the shop with the rest of the white guys he made a statement--- and he didn't care about me hearing him. He said, "Somebody needs to tell that boy he's a Nigger". In his mind, all he could see me doing was working out back in the shop washing and cleaning vehicles. But I had other ideas and dreams.

I knew at that point, I was not making enough money to do the things I wanted to do in life. I wanted to be a mechanic. Working there, I knew the guy I was working under was not going to allow me to learn a lot about mechanics. He'd let me take a vehicle apart, but when it came time to put it back together, I had a vehicle to wash, or something to clean or trash to haul away. I knew I had to get away from there. I knew I had to do better.

The driving force in my determination to do better was the fact they never expected me to do anything but wash vehicles out back of the shop and do whatever they told me to do. They made a big thing out of the fact somebody forgot to tell me that I was a nigger. That hurt me, but it was not going to break me. It gave me more of a desire to save and get out of that place. I was determined I would do better for myself. With that in mind, I stayed there and worked a good while longer. The next summer an incident happened when a load of pipe came in from down in Lufkin, Texas. It was a Friday evening and all of the help was gone except me and the bosses. The only reason the boss was still there was because I was washing his pickup. It had been such a busy day; I had not cleaned his truck for the weekend. I was doing this when the truck pulled up with a load of pipe.

I had been operating what we called a gin pole truck on the yard. It had a boom on the back and could pick up a very heavy load. One boss was in the back waiting for me to finish with his truck and the other boss was out front in the store. The boss I worked directly for told the other one he would go by one of the other workers house and pick him up and, "McArthur can bring the gin pole truck out there and we can get that pipe unloaded." In order to unload the pipe, I would have to operate the gin pole truck. There was a strip cable hooked to each end of the pipe and I'd pick it up and a tag line would keep the pipe from spinning around. There was going to be two white men, one on each end of the pipe. I would pick it up with the truck and put it on the rack. We would have to repeat that process until the entire pipe was unloaded. The guy I worked for told the other boss he would get a couple of guys and I could bring the gin pole truck and we could get the pipe unloaded. The other guy told my boss, "You can't do that." He said, "Yes we can. McArthur is going to operate the truck and I'll get two other fellows to help him." He again said, "You can't do that." My boss asked, "Why can't we?" He answered, "You mean you're going to have two white men on the ground and *him* operating the truck?" "Yes, that's what I'm going to do." He again said, "You can't do that." My boss asked," why?" He said, "Because he's a nigger."

That was said in front of me and the truck driver. They had no problem using that word loosely.

Let me tell you about the guy who said that somebody forgot to tell me that I was a nigger. He was pretty liberal, but back in those days a white man could not be seen being too friendly with a black. White people would give him a hard time for being nice to whom they called a nigger. I knew in my heart the guy I worked directly for was a pretty decent guy, because I'd seen him on several occasions when the whites would come on the lot when I was washing a vehicle and try to pick at me. I couldn't do anything about it because in those days you'd better not talk back to a white man. All they would have to say is "That nigger got smart with me." Then you would have five or six other whites picking to see if you'd get smart with them. The next thing you knew, someone had jumped on you. If someone jumped on you, there was no law enforcement on your side. All you had was the boss and if he didn't come to your rescue, you definitely did not call the police. If you called the police on a white man, he was going to get there and whip your head. If a white man slapped you or kicked you, the first thing the policeman wanted to know was "What did *you* do?" A white man was never going to be wrong. It was always something you did or said to cause him to react in that manner. So what you had to do was look at them, maybe grin, nod your head and say, "yes sir, yes sir", and try not to irritate them. If you did, life would be harder for you. If he didn't do anything to you, he would turn other white folks on you. They would see if you'd talk back to them, so they could have an opportunity to torture you.

~

That reinforced to me things had to change. I told myself, "You will never get the things you want here." That next fall I left and went to Dallas, Texas. I had a couple of friends who had already moved to Dallas and were working. So I decided to give Dallas a try. I was able to get a job working at a hotel washing dishes. I was determined, so I worked at this hotel by night and went to school by day. I enrolled in Lincoln Technical Institute in Dallas, because my dream was to become a mechanic. I wanted to be a mechanic because if I was a good mechanic I could have a good, stable income and could have the things in life I wanted.

After graduating from Lincoln Tech, I went to Detroit, Michigan. That's where they make those cars. I got a job in Detroit at a dealership. I had finally made it to the big time. I had a job at a dealership where I could work on new cars and didn't have to work on junk. I worked there for a number of years before I was drafted. I was drafted in 1967 and went into service. I ended up in Vietnam. I survived Vietnam, came home, and went back to my old job. I worked there a number of years before I decided to move back to South Arkansas.   I moved back to the same area where I was born and reared.   I had heard all my life about how liberal white people were in the North. There are some good ones all over. But at that time, you still needed to know how to work with them and how to get along. I decided it was not much better than south Arkansas.

$$\smallsmile$$

I then got my second job. I lived out of one check and saved the other one for five years. I returned to south Arkansas with the same determination to be an auto mechanic and build me a shop. Things had gotten a little better. Not a whole lot, but a little better. I took my money, bought a piece of property and built me a service station, an Exxon station. Still determined to have something in life, I ran the service station for twelve years. I got bored with the station. I was doing mechanic work, but was still not satisfied. I closed the station and went to work for a chemical company as a mechanic. I was classified as an industrial mechanic. I've worked there for twenty years. I have reached retirement age but I'm doing what I really like to do. I love this job. I'm 66 years old now and still working.

I can truthfully tell you what has put me where I am was having a strong determination. I have always seen white people having nice homes and property and those were the things I wanted. I was willing to work to have those things, but it was so hard to get a job making the kind of money to afford those things in this area. A lot of people in my area would have more than what they have if the jobs had been available. But if the jobs are not there, you're not going to have very much, making small change.

Just because you don't have the job you want or make the kind of money you want, you can't let that be a stopping point to keep you from reaching your dreams.

I was making $35 a week when I worked at the service station washing cars and hauling trash and doing all the things that they told me to do. Out of that $35 I gave my sisters $2-3 a week to take care of my clothes. They would have done it anyway as a part of family duty. All they really wanted was enough to buy hair oil, deodorant and personal items. I also gave my mother $5 a week. I know that was not much, but back in the 60's it helped with things she needed around the house. I saved the rest of my check.

I walked five miles to work. I'd get up in the morning and begin my walk and sometimes someone down the road with a car would stop and give me a ride. In those days I was young and energetic and could make the trip in 45 minutes.

Occasionally, when there was no one else in the store, I would go in and trade my ones and fives for a couple of twenty dollar bills. I actually saved money, making only $35 a week. At that time I had no habits. I just had a desire to achieve something in life.

My father was always interested in my saving money. He had a philosophy. He would say, "Son, you'll never have anything if you start out fresh every Monday morning. If you're waiting to get paid, you must have just gotten that job." He said, "If a man is ever going to have anything, he must find a way to live out of less than he makes." In today's world people will tell you that's hard. But I am drawn to labor and I will tell my kids, your kids and anybody else's kids to learn to live out of less than you make, no matter how little you make. Anybody who makes enough to live, makes enough to save. There is always something you can do, even if you have to put quarters in a jug. If you put quarters in a jug long enough, you will eventually have to get another jug because that one will be full.

That same philosophy proved true to me when I was making $35 a week. Every now and then I'd have to go into the store because my wallet would become so full until it was hard to fold. When that happened, I'd have to exchange my ones and fives for twenty dollar bills. With the help of God I was lifted from nothing— one poor, nappy headed, brogan shoe, patched overall wearing kid --- from nowhere to somewhere.

I say any man that makes enough to live, makes enough to save. You just have to ask yourself, "How bad do I want it?" If you want it bad enough, you will find a way.

When I told that man that I was going to have a house with a two-car garage---I built that house! It was only 1800 sq. ft., but it was built. The house had a two-car garage, two living rooms (well they call them dens nowadays), but it had two sitting rooms. That was one of the things in life that I promised myself I was going to save my money and do, and I built that house. I bought property just like I said I was going to do. I now live in my third house. I built the first one, had the second one build, and bought the third one already built. I had already bought the 40 acres of land that adjourns the property that my third house sits on. That house sits on 20 acres that joined the 40 acres I already owned so now I live on a 60-acre tract. I was able to design the landscape of my farm myself. The person I bought the house and 20 acres from had it in trees. I wanted it to look like a park. I had the unwanted trees taken out, planted grass and fenced the entire 60 acres. I built the fence so that my cows could come up to the house. The property is shaped like a horseshoe with the house sitting in the center. The cows can come up to the house on either side or behind. There was a pond already behind the house on the property. The property has a lane from the highway that leads to the house. Everything about it fits my design, so it was prefect to add to what I already had.

I have worked for everything that I have. Nobody has given me anything. That comes from starting out in life on my own with nothing. If I can do that, I have a problem understanding why other people can't make a commitment to pull themselves up and stay between the two laws – the law of man and the law of God. If you can work and save and plan to pull yourself up from whatever situation you are dissatisfied with, you can. But you have to ask yourself – How bad do I want it? It takes time, commitment and a belief in God, but it can be done.

THAT KIND OF STUFF

I LOOK AT the younger generation – young Black men espe-
cially, getting lost by the wayside. My brother Grady drives a
street bus in Detroit, Michigan. He told me one day there was
a lady who rode his bus all the way to the end of the line, and
back. He was about to begin his route again when he noticed
this same lady was still on the bus. He had a few minutes to rest
before he began his next route. He began to talk with the lady
and she told him she had seen her last son go to prison that day.
She was very upset because she had lost her last son. She began to tell him, "I carried my boys to all of the amusement parks,
I even carried them down south to visit their relatives and I gave
them everything I could and I still lost my boys to prison." Being a
minister he asked her, "Did you ever carry them to church?" She
said, "No, we never had time for that kind of stuff."

My thinking on that situation is a lot of us are letting our boys
go because we don't have time for that kind of stuff. They are 12,
13 and 14 years old – a most critical time in their lives – and we will
go to the church and leave them at home asleep because they
didn't want to go to church. Well just like *somebody forgot to tell
me that I was Black*, someone forgot to tell them that everyone
has a right to life and a right to exist. When you hurt one person
you hurt a lot of other people. When you hurt one young man,
that young man has a mother, father, brothers, sisters, aunts and
uncles. You hurt everybody in that family that cares about him.
Somebody forgot to tell those boys they should not grow up in this

world with the philosophy that I'm going to do unto them before they do unto me. Somebody forgot to teach them how to get along in the world. Somebody forgot to teach them how to go out in the world and still live a decent life without committing a lot of crimes.

I said before there's the law of man and there's the law of God. Someone forget to tell them they have to obey the law, but that is why I'm a strong believer in the military. Because a lot of our young men grow up never having to obey any form of authority. So when they grow up and hit the streets they are guaranteed to go to jail and end up in prison because mother, father, or whoever was guardian of them forgot to tell them they had to stay between the two laws.

We've taken the church out of everything and that's one of our greatest downfalls. It has hurt everyone. All of these young men that are committing crimes and going to jail and prison are a burden on society. It's hurting our whole society because now there is a young man you have to support for 20, 30, or 40 years in prison. All because somebody didn't have time for that kind of stuff. Somebody should have told them, to become a success in life; you must learn to live between the two laws. When you start breaking the two laws, you are headed for destruction. The law of man and the law of God are pretty much parallel. So it is of utmost importance that we live by both laws.

I don't understand how a young man can grow up and think he is smarter than the law. He thinks he can commit crime and be smart enough not to get caught. No one is smarter than the law. Every lie he can tell, every trick in the book, the law has already heard.

There are those families who allow their children to go out and get things and bring them home. When you haven't given him money and he doesn't have a job, but you allow him to bring home things you know he couldn't afford. You can turn a blind eye to that and I guarantee you are going to visit him in jail.

I've been reasonably successful in life and I probably could have had more than what I have, but I've learned to live by the two laws and stay within the two laws. I'm 66 years old and have never spent time in jail or prison thank God. I've even wanted to go inside a jail to see how it feels to be in jail. I've heard it's not a pleasant feeling. It goes back to what I said earlier, "How bad do you want it?" How bad do you want to be free? How bad do you want to be a success in life? You have to ask yourself that question.

One can say a lot of things when we are growing up and shooting the breeze with the other guys. But when you live your life, what you say can be quiet, but what you do speaks so loud, until others really don't hear what you say.

THE SIMPLE LIFE

WHEN I WAS a child growing up, we did not have electricity in our house, not even in our community. Therefore we did not have a television and for lights we had kerosene lamps. My mother had a big bible and instead of sitting and watching television or playing video games, my mother read to us the bible. When reading to us, my mother would stop and explain things that were in the bible, what she had just read and what it meant.

I believe that quality time with the family has stayed with us throughout our lives. It instilled in us very high morals and taught us that we must live by those two laws.

My father was the Chief Word in our home. When he said bedtime, everybody got right up and put their bed clothes on and went to bed. We would take turns taking a bath in the big metal tub. In the summer we would set the water in the sun and let the sun heat the bathwater. The girls would be in one room taking a bath and the boys would be in another room. Mom and Dad would sit on the porch and talk until we were finished with our baths.

In the winter we sat around the wood stove. My mother would be reading to us and my father would be talking. When my children were born I tried to instill those same family values in them.

COW FEVER

I AM NOT negative of the Caucasian race; because I owe some of my success to them, they have helped me a lot. I raise cows on my farm today. I was encouraged by a white friend of the family. Mr. Mack Pratt had been a friend of the family since I was a small child. He and my dad were acquaintances. They would meet up at the store and have things to talk about, crops, kids, animals and stuff. So he encouraged me to try and raise cows. I tried it and I like raising cows. I'm by no means a big cattle grower, but I enjoy the small herd. Although growing up as a child, I didn't like working with cows at all, because they were a lot of work. We had milk cows and we had to take care of them, with all of the milking and feeding. I wasn't really that excited about cows until I was grown and I bought my first piece of land and this gentleman suggested that I raise cows. I bought my first two heifer calves from the sale barn. I raised them up and took them to his farm to be breed. I didn't even have a bull. The following year the two cows had calves. My whole cow herd was started with those two cows. The next year I had one bull and one heifer calf. I sold the bull and kept the heifer. But the next year I was able to buy my own bull. I got my start with land ownership from white people. When I came back home from Viet Nam, I was looking to buy a piece of land. Another white gentleman, who had been a family friend, suggested I buy a small piece that belonged to his sister which was cut off from a larger piece of land by the main highway. She had no use for it because it was such a small piece of land on the wrong side of the highway. I bought that small piece of land and built my second house and shop. The lady had told her brother when she passed on to sell me the rest of the land because I already bought that little piece on the wrong side of the road. So when she died, he came to me and told me what she had said and told me I had first choice to buy the land. So later, my wife Mary, and I bought the larger piece of land. We then had land on both sides of the highway.

It was the help of those white gentlemen which gave me the opportunity to get involved with something I truly love. I love working with cows, they don't lie on me, don't steal from me and don't cheat on me. I can go on the farm on Saturday and piddle around all day long and at the end of the day, those cows don't go back and tell my wife anything I said or did. I can spend my money on them and get a good return. When my wife tells me she needs something I can put four or five of them in the lot and call the cow hauler, he will take them to the sale barn and they in return will mail me a check. Those old cows are good to me, and I just like working with them. I am considered a hobby farmer. I still work my job at the chemical plant where I am an industrial mechanic. I work with my cows in my spare time. I'll take a week of vacation and cut and bale hay.

There's another black man, Eugene White, who lives down the road from me and he also owns cows. He and I now work together. I don't charge him when I work on his farm and he doesn't charge me when he works on my farm. We cut and bale hay and build fences together. We welded pipe fences on both our farms and I am very proud of those fences.

CHILDREN

THAT BRINGS UP the subject of how we look at the success of our children. You really shouldn't judge one child against the other. We all are different individuals with our strong points and weaknesses. We all have different levels at which we perform and we have different levels at which we will be successful. When I was raising my children I always expected the best out of each one of them, but I never compared one child's performance against the other because they were all different. So when you start talking about your success versus your friends they will also be different.

There was a piece of family land for sale. One of my aunts had some land she wanted to sale and I wanted to buy it real bad. But my mother told me Mac, you already have a pretty good piece of land, why don't you hold up and let your brother buy that tract of land. Well at that time it seem like one of the worst ideas ever, to back off and let one of my younger brothers buy the property. It just didn't seem fair that my mother would ask that of me knowing that I was already trying to raise cows and needed all the land I could possibly buy. My brother lived way out west in a great big Western California city. What in God's name would he do with this country land? Absolutely nothing. So I backed off and let him buy it, but at the time I really thought Mom had pulled a little favoritism on me there.

Years later a piece of property came up for sale joining the property I already owned. Obeying my mother put me in position to buy that piece of property that I most desperately needed. Because I didn't buy the first piece of land, I still had my money and was able to buy the piece that joined my property. It goes back to obeying your parents. I didn't see it at the time, but the Lord worked it out to be one of the best decisions I ever made.

It goes back to what I was saying earlier; obey the two laws; the law of God and the law of man. Yes, that was the law of God, obey your mother and father, and I did. I tell you I can't think of a time when I obeyed my mother and father and it didn't turn out for my good.

FATHER'S DREAM

DURING WORLD WAR II my Dad served at a Naval Base in California. I grew up as a child sitting on the front porch in the summer and by the heater in the winter, listening to my dad talk about his military days in California. He always wanted to buy a good car and carry all of us, his family to California. He wanted his family to see what the countryside looked like between Arkansas and California. He talked about that until he'd gotten old and then he began to talk about how he wished he would have done that, taken his family on that trip.

When I grew up and had a family, I would take my family on a trip every summer. Some of the best vacations we ever had were when we didn't go anyplace in particular. We just got in the car and turned left or right out of the driveway and said let's just go yonder way. We would drive during the day, take in the countryside and sights, then about dark we would get a hotel, freshen up, eat, rest, sleep and be ready to go the next day. My purpose, for that type of vacation, was because if I had called a family member in St. Louis and said I was leaving home at 6:00, in ten hours or so they would be looking for me. That put me on a time schedule, which took all the fun out of our unplanned, unrestricted vacation. We loved the freedom to change our minds, even change course if we wanted. When my children read about certain locations, most of the stateside stuff, I had already carried them to those places.

One year we drove out of the driveway, of course I live on a major highway, and we decided to go east and follow this highway. We ended up at Myrtle Beach and we put our feet in the Atlantic Ocean on the east coast. We then said let's just follow this up the coast; we ended up in New York. We would sight see by day and stop at night to rest. We stopped in South Carolina, North Carolina, Richmond, Virginia; we went on to the Capitol and toured Washington, D. C. A couple ships had docked and been made into museums and we toured them along the way. Once in New York, we went to see the Statue of Liberty, Times Square and downtown New York, New York, over the Bridge into Northern New York. We then drove from Northern New York into Canada and there   we saw Niagara Falls. We toured Niagara Falls, drove on from Canada over to Michigan, and came across the Ambassador Bridge into Detroit. We then turned around and drove back through the tunnel then came back over the Bridge into Detroit where we have relatives. We visited with them for a few days then we got a map and plotted a course back home.

We have also taken several western vacations. On one in particular was when we took the Southern route, went down to Houston, on over to San Antonio, down to Big Bend National Park and on to Tucson, Arizona. We ended up at the San Diego Zoo.

On another trip we left home, went over to Oklahoma, up through Kansas and took the northern route up through the Bad Lands over to Mount Rushmore and up to Yellowstone National Park. The sights were breathtaking. We left Yellowstone on the West Gate, still headed west. We went into Oregon and visited Crater Lake, came down out of Oregon traveling Highway 101 and came into Northern California. We were speechless when we entered the Redwood Forest. The trees had our necks aching, they were so huge. We even took a picture of one of the trees with our car driven right through the center of the tree. Still traveling the famous Coastal Highway, we took a brief stop and visited one of the beautiful beaches and wet our feet in the Pacific

Ocean. We traveled most of that day along the coast. We went through a very long tunnel and when we exited ---Wow! There it was, the *Golden Gate Bridge*. We spent a half day looking at the Bay. We got the sight of our lives when we observed wild seals in the Bay on a small island. We crossed the Bridge and drove through downtown San Francisco. We then crossed over into Oakland and we began our descent back home. We came back by way of the Grand Canyon and then made our way on home.

I guess all of this was a fulfillment of a dream. My dad always dreamed of returning to California with us, his family, and never did, so I felt every trip I made was in fulfillment of his dream. His dream for us became a reality for me and my family. Because of our adventures, most of the major sights my children read about in school, they amazed their teachers and peers when they would say, "We've been there".

Sometimes the kids would say, "I don't believe you", and they would just come home and get the picture albums and carry them back and show our vacation pictures.

Well, all the kids are grown now and all but one have started their own lives with their families fulfilling their dreams, traveling with their families just as I traveled with them.

Now for me, I try to live a simple life, busying myself around the farm. My wife also tries to live a common, simple life. She's a musician; she plays the piano and also the organ. She teaches piano lessons at our home. She has a number of students who come once a week for lessons. At the end of the year she has a recital, which is the highlight of her year. She has a fun day after her recital to reward her students and their families. They are all invited out to the farm. We provide the food for a big cookout. We have a pond and everyone fishes in the morning. Then the cook crew, which consists of me and my children, clean the fish and cook them and add them to the menu. We all eat and then the kids swim and we end up the day with a nature tour of the farm. My wife plays at the church and sometimes other local churches when needed. We both participate and support the church. I believe in God. I believe in God with my whole heart and soul. I do not believe you can be all you can be or be the success that you want to be without belief in God. I don't advocate any specific religion. I think a person should go to a church where he's comfortable, enjoy and feel that he's getting what he needs. I don't feel like a person should go to a church where he doesn't want to be, but I do feel that one should attend some form of service. That's just my belief.

BACK TO UNITY

IN MY HOMETOWN, which I guess is no more that a wide place in the road, there is not even a red light because every time one is installed someone shoots it out. Before the Civil Rights Movement there were two Black barber shops, a Black dry cleaner and out at the edge of the countryside there was a black man who had a store and a gas pump. There was more unity among Black people in our area at that time. We went through the Civil Rights movement and we joined together; but after that movement, we all have gone our separate ways. We are not bond by much of anything but the church. No I'm not a preacher, don't want to be, never have been, would have been but the Lord didn't call me. I think my calling was to live my life and write this book.

But after the Civil Rights movement, we stopped supporting each other, we got better jobs, better cars, better homes and the opportunity to enter into forbidden places, the once segregated white establishment and we abandoned our own businesses. Everyone started going their own separate way. We forgot about the small mom and pop stores that used to be our lifeline.

In the next town, which was a little larger, they had three Black hotels. The civil rights movement changed a lot of things and thank God for it, but all I'm saying is when we obtained our freedom to go where we please, we deserted the small Black businesses. When we did this we gave a signal to our youth, don't try to have your own business, because we are not going to support you.

I was very fortunate. I built a service station shortly after the civil rights movement around 1970. I was an Exxon dealer. After the first five years or so following the civil rights movement of the mid 60's, my business did really good. Everyone was excited about a young Black man in business for himself in that era. But years on into my business career, a lot of my Black customers stopped supporting, for various reasons, but the White customers continued. I ran my service station for 12 years, and I didn't close because I wasn't making any money, but I needed more benefits than I could afford as an independent station owner. I had a young family with needs, dental insurance, medical insurance and retirement for myself --- all of the things that the bigger companies had to offer. So I closed my service station and went to work at the Chemical Plant. I soon learned the value of benefits while raising a young family. Thankfully my family grew up and are all doing well. Three of my five children have college degrees from Grambling State University. Two have Masters and one is almost a PhD. My youngest son, although he didn't choose college, went to a prestigious welding school, Tulsa Welding, and is a master welder. All thank Goodness are well and free and have never seen the inside of a jail cell. Well, except my youngest, who when he first went to work at age 19 after finishing welding school and began to make more money than he ever dreamed of, thought he was rich and that a checking account never ran out. That is until he wrote one too many checks that his account couldn't cover and ended up spending a night in jail to get his attention. But that's the only problem we have had with the law.

I encourage my children to spend quality time with their families. One of my daughters took her kids to Disney World for Spring break, my son who is in Washington, D. C. and works for the Federal Government travels a lot on his job. He and his wife travel in their spare time also. I have five granddaughters and one grandson. I am very proud of all of them. I have one granddaughter who is almost finished at Grambling State University. My wife graduated from Grambling and I finished from Lincoln Technical School and I am very proud of my trade school training also.

I don't dare promise you that if you go to college or to a trade school that you will be the success that you want to be, but I can promise you if you don't go to college or a trade school, you won't ever have a chance to be all you can be. Just think about this, why should a company hire you and train you, when there's ten people in line with you who have already been to school and are much more knowledgeable than you? It's like buying a car. Why should you buy a car with a one gallon gas tank when there's one with a 20 gallon gas tank? You can drive for miles and miles without stopping, versus the one with a one gallon gas tank where every 10 to 20 miles you have to stop and put in more gas. I made that comparison to show that if you are untrained, your capacity to perform will not be comparable to someone who is educated and trained for the job. Your chance of getting the good jobs, making the money you deserve is just not going to happen without a proper education.

OUT WEST

LET ME TELL you about a trip we took out west. It was one of the scariest trips I guess we ever experienced. We stopped at the Bad Lands and we were touring the sights of the land left from erosion, the canyons and ravine. We stopped at this location and my older son went down into one of those canyons. My baby son took off running back toward the car, we thought. But when we got back to the car he had gone past the car, still running. There was a walking trail that was about three miles or so around this particular area. My youngest son thought he could just go around to the back side of the hill and get down into the canyon where his older brother was, not realizing that all the canyons look alike and the back side of that canyon could have been 20 miles or more away. We could see his little head darting on the trail running in the opposite direction so my older son and I started running and calling to him to stop. He already had a big head start on us; it's about 1 o'clock in the afternoon, already extremely hot. I knew I could not catch a 7 or 8 year old running that fast. It was up to my oldest son to save the day. My older son was younger, so he got close enough for him to hear him calling and got him to stop. We all got back to the car and rested and talked about how tragic that incident could have become because there is so much uncharted area in the Bad Lands. We were just grateful we caught our little speed demon that day.

We went on all the way up to the Black Hills and I realized why they are called black. They really look black when you are driving toward them, but when you get to the hills you realize the black appearance is pine trees. They are so green that they look black from a distance. We were high up in the mountains and we stopped at a crossroad town where two interstates intersected. We got a motel for the night. We were still way out west. We got our room and the kids wanted to go swimming. It was still early evening; there was an outside pool which we could see from the room balcony, so I didn't mind. I noticed that the hotel clerk had given us a lot of extra blankets and towels. The pool had about 20 or more people in it so when our kids went down; they just got in the pool. No one said anything out of the way, but when my three children went in; in five minutes they had a private pool. All the white people got out. They gave them that pool. I noticed one little child was crying, "No Mom, we just got in", but she was yanking on that kid's arm and pulling him to their room. My kids didn't think anything about it at first. They played for maybe an hour and came back to the room. I looked back out there 30 or 40 minutes later and all the white people had gotten back in the pool. My kids then noticed, "You know when we went down to swim all the white people got out, we had the pool all to ourselves." They watched TV for awhile and they later wanted to go swim some more. Well, I noticed this time when we stepped on the balcony all eyes were on us. As my kids went down the walkway all eyes were on them. They got into the pool and in about 5 minutes the same thing happened again. My kids were then aware of what was going on and they came back to the room saying, "Mom and Dad, do you want to see the white people flee?" I then understood why they gave us all the extra supplies, so we wouldn't come back out of the room. But to our good fortune, no one said or did anything to us. They just moved and got away from us as if we were contagious. The next morning we checked-out and gassed up. On down the road, I asked a service station attendant if there were any Black people living in those parts. She said, "Well no, there are no, ah, there are not any, ah Black people." She said it real slow, like she was afraid to use the word black. So then I knew why the hotel clerk had given us so many extra supplies, so we would stay in our room. Then I realized that in about three days we hadn't seen any other Black people anywhere.

We pulled into a roadside park just before dark. Now I'm aware that there are no other black people around here in these parts. So my two boys decided they would do some exploring. Me, my wife and daughter went to the restroom and came back to the car, but not the boys, they were nowhere to be found. We're in a mega sized roadside park, filled with cars, trucks, RV's, big rigs, and hundreds of people, none of whom I know or who know me, and my two boys are missing. I began to panic; I had gotten into the car to go down and block the exit and shut everything down until I found my boys. Just as I started the car, I saw them coming back through the fence. With all the walking trails and sidewalks, they had gone over the fence to explore the outer areas of the park. Now that's my boys!

That was one of the scariest times I remember in our travels. We have traveled from the east coast to the west, from the northern United States into Canada, and Southern United States into Mexico; from the Atlantic to the Pacific from Mackintosh Straits to the Gulf of Mexico. We have seen a lot of these United States from New York to Los Angeles, from Muskegon, Michigan to New Orleans, from Yellowstone to Big Bend, from Crater Lake to the Grand Canyon, from Hoover Dam to the Mississippi River, yes, we have covered a lot of this country. But with all of the trips, I would still like to pick up Highway 10 and run it all the way to San Diego and then travel to Northern California on Highway 101 back into Oregon and back over to Yellowstone and come on back home from that direction. But if that never happens, I can still say we have traveled well these United States.

I have some great pictures and some great memories and I have found that the people of these United States are basically the same allover. You may like a particular area for the sights and other personal reasons, but when you start dealing with the people, from the east coast to the west coast, they are basically the same. They are like the trees in the forest, some are bigger, some are taller, some are wider, some are shorter, some are fatter, some are skinner, but in general, people throughout the United States have shown me to be pretty much the same all over. You are going to find some good ones and you will find some just as bad as they come.

I have always told my kids that if you are out there, something can happen to you. You don't have to be doing anything wrong, but just in the wrong place at the wrong time. So if you are out there something can happen to you. There is trouble around every corner. That's why I used to tell my boys if you're at home you can't be involved with what happened at the club. So always be careful

TRUCKING COMPANY

WHEN I FINISHED school at Lincoln Tech in Dallas, I had two reasons why I didn't want to stay in Dallas. One was the police department in those days. They could stop a young Black man walking down the street anytime and interrogate him for no reason. They would just stop and ask "Where are you going? Where have you been? Show me some identification, what are you doing in this area? I didn't like that. I was from South Arkansas, living deep in the country, so I'd never encountered policemen that were that rude.

The other reason was I worked at a trucking company, doing cleaning on transmission and parts which were taken out of the trucks. I would put them on a dolly and roll them out back and put them on a pad. I would steam them off, clean them up and this, that or the other. One evening I had worked on one that they were going to replace some gears in and I was to clean it up and take the top off of it and clean it out. It had heavy, heavy oil inside. Before I got off work that night, I had wrestled it back up on the dolly. Overnight the heat from the hot water had heated up the transmission and it seeped some more oil and it had settled in the bottom of the transmission. I knew I had done a good job on washing and cleaning, so I didn't really inspect it, I just rolled it into the shop the next morning so it could be worked on by one of the mechanics. He got it and set it up on his work table. When he began to work, he saw oil had seeped out into the bottom, not much, but a little oil was present. So he walked to the back door and called me. He didn't have to go through the boss. I was the only Black guy working there and I worked out back anyway. Well all of the White guys felt like they could order me around and tell me what they wanted to tell me. In some way they felt like they too were my boss. So he stepped out the door and called me to come back in and get that transmission out of there and get it clean. I made the statement, "When I get my promotion and I get up in here and start working on transmissions, I am not going to be that hard to please." He stopped me dead in my tracks. He said, "Look here, you're never going to come up in the shop with us and work on anything." He didn't use the same words that the guy had used years before, but he made it very clear. He said, "Just look at yourself, look at who you are, Freddy will never let you come up in here and work on anything." "You're doing the only thing you gonna ever do. You're gonna wash and clean, keep the floors swept up and do that type work, but you ain't never gonna come up in this shop and call yourself working on something with us, you hear me?"

That was one of the reasons I had that burning desire to leave Dallas. Because I still wanted things in life and I knew working a second class job the rest of my life was not going to get me where I needed to be. I didn't quit that day. I stayed on the job, but that confirmed Dallas was not the place where I wanted to live. That helped me make up my mind I was moving to Detroit. I had better luck in Detroit. A few days later, it might have been a week later, it was lunchtime and two men who worked near the back of the shop near the back door were putting a front shaft in a transmission. They were going to put the needle bearings in it and I stepped in the back door to watch them. A couple of guys had already washed their hands and were eating their lunch. These two guys wanted to get that front shaft in the transmission before they stopped to eat lunch. It was lunch time. It wasn't like I was supposed to be out back working and I wasn't, it was my free time. I stepped in the back door of the shop and was watching them assemble the gear so they could put the front shaft in there. I guess I would have been alright if I had just stood there and kept quiet, but I asked one of the guys, he was pretty friendly toward me, so I asked him, "How are you all going to get all those little ole bearings to say in that front shaft while you put it in?" That's when the boss walked over to about where they were. The guy was telling me, we are going to put heavy grease on them and they will stay in place while we put it in the transmission. That's all he got a chance to tell me. The boss walked up there and started chewing on my butt and a butt chewing that lasted about three minutes. He must have called me boy at least ten times--- "Boy you don't work in this shop." "Boy I didn't hire you to work in this shop." "Boy if I catch you back up in this shop bothering these mechanics again, you are going to have to find yourself a new job." He went on and on and on. Then he pointed to the back door and said, "In fact you get your butt on back out there." But it was lunch time. So I walked back out the back door and I walked all the way around to the front of the shop. I guess those guys knew how bad he had hurt my feelings. They were standing in the front door looking at me as I left there walking. In fact I was so hurt from that butt chewing that I must have walked ten blocks before I even thought about catching a bus. I had a couple of sandwiches lying on the shelf out back in the doghouse (that was just a little building where they kept spare parts and where I was allowed to eat my lunch). I was so hurt that I didn't even get my sandwiches. So I went on and caught a bus. That was on a Wednesday. I never went back. In fact to this day they still owe me for 2-1/2 days work that I never went back to receive. That was how and why I left my job at the trucking company.

It was sometime around January coming up on February. I'm on my way to Detroit, but I didn't want to go out there right then because it gets cold out there and they have lots and lots or snow. I didn't want to go out there while it was still winter. So I got another job and kicked around Dallas, at least until the first of summer. I walked around the rest of that week until I found a man that had three stores and he needed a stocker. I thought about that job over night, and decided, any piece of job would do until summer, as long as I could make some decent money to take care of myself and have a little bit left over. So I took the stocker job. He had three food shops, Food Shop #1, 2, and 3. What I would do is start at Store #1. He had a worker already and a pick-up truck. We would do what we needed to do at #1 then we would get in the truck and go to #2. We would walk the aisles and see what we needed, then we would go in the back room with a 4-wheel dolly, load it up and come out and start stocking. The other guy always liked the cosmetic section. After about a week, I pretty well knew what to do, so I would come into the store, he would start talking to the cashier and I would go on in the back room after I completed my survey. I would go in the back, load my supplies on the dolly and begin stocking. I got to where I was doing all the work and he would just hang around looking at the cosmetics or up front talking to the check out lady. It wasn't that bad of a job, it was clean and basically inside. I kind of liked that job alright, but it was not paying what I needed in order to do the things I wanted to do. I stayed there and worked until almost springtime since my intentions were to leave that job anyway. Then I found out that the boss was paying me $3 an hour less than this White guy and he wasn't doing any work. He was just driving me from store to store and I did all the work. I wasn't satisfied with the pay situation, so I stayed on with them until the spring and then I left that job also. I gave it up. I gave up Dallas.

I went back to El Dorado and stayed around a while before moving on to Detroit.

DETROIT

BACK WHEN I was a boy, we had 3rd Sunday in August Church Meeting, known as "Homecoming". All the people that had moved away would plan their vacation so they could come home at that time to be with their families and friends. That was a big thing. People from all around would converge on the church grounds on that day. Our church was a very large white wooden church and it held a very large crowd for those days. But all the people that came on that day could not get inside; the majority would be on the outside. The windows would be raised and people would stand outside near the windows just to hear what was going on in the church. When collection was taken up, two or three of the deacons would come outside with hats and take up money from the people on the outside of the church. They would take the money back inside and dump it on the table. They would sometime take up more money from the outside than they would on the inside.

When church was over and everyone was dispersing to their individual forms of transportation, my dad would stand near his truck. Now if you were a young person, you would go near your vehicle and wait until the older people were ready to go. My dad was standing not too far from our truck talking to another man about farming, or planting crops. They were standing out there just talking. There was a lady who had a little baby about three months old. She walked up to my dad and said you ain't seen my baby yet, and just shoved her baby in my dad's arm, just pushed it right into his arms. My daddy had no choice—either take the baby or let it fall. Once she had pushed the baby into my dad's arms, she took about two steps back and started talking to the both of them. She was enjoying talking to those men; meanwhile my dad was still holding this baby in his arms. Well, my mama was all the way across the church yard, my daddy could see her coming his way. This lady had her back to my mama and she was busy talking to them. Now my daddy's standing there like a statue, holding this baby out from his chest, he knew not to embrace the baby. My daddy is looking at my mother coming in his direction and he can't move. He knew this was not good. My mama walked on up, took the baby out of his arms. She looked at the baby and told the lady, here, you have a fine baby, while passing the baby back to the lady.

Now my dad had done nothing wrong, the lady pushed the baby right into his arms, but my mother didn't know that. She saw my daddy holding another woman's baby an that just didn't set well with her. But on the way home ... We kids had to ride in the back of the truck, the bigger kids on a board across the back behind the cab and the rest of us on the floor of the truck bed. My mama yang, yang, and fussed at my daddy all the way home. We got home and he hurried up and got out of those church clothes and put on some work clothes and made a bee line to the potato house to get away from that nagging woman. When I went to bed that night my mama was still raising sand at my daddy. I woke up the next morning, we had breakfast, she got us kids out of the house by telling us, "Ya'll get out of here and go play". This was early in the morning. Normally my mama and daddy tried not to have disagreements before us kids, but she was too mad to follow the rules this time. It really didn't matter who was listening, she was tearing him up and he really hadn't done anything wrong. Well needless to say, I was about 14 and I knew he was totally innocent. My mama fussed him out that whole week. I said right then, "Lord I pray that I don't get a woman like that." Now don't get me wrong, my mama was a good woman, but Lord she was really upset. You can see why I'm the way I am.   I can take criticism, I can take being corrected, but I will not tolerate constant nagging.   There again, I had to get away from this.

Back in those days kids didn't get in grown folks business. No matter how innocent my daddy was, and I knew it, I couldn't say a word. If my mother had asked me something then I could have told what I knew, but other than that, you kept your mouth shut. You just did not get in grown folks affairs. You were not allowed to get in grown folks conversations. All I could do was to listen and sympathize with my daddy.

Well I'm ready to leave Dallas. I came home so I could see my mama before going to Detroit. Detroit was much farther away than Dallas and I was ready to make my fortune. I came back to my home town of El Dorado, Arkansas, but I actually live closer to Strong, Arkansas, so I claim them both. I attended school in Strong, so I guess Strong is my hometown. It's not a really big place, in fact today we don't even have a stop light, just a wide place in the road, some stores and a few hundred people live there. But it's a real good town, with real good folks.

Well I'm getting ready to go to Detroit. When I got there, Detroit was good to me. I had a sister who lived in Detroit at that time, my oldest sister, an aunt and several other kin people.   I lived with my sister for a short period of time. Then I went down to the local board and registered for the draft. That was mandatory. Each time you moved you had to go to the local board and register because we were actively in the middle of the Viet Nam War.

I was very lucky and got a job right away. I worked at a car dealership as a line mechanic. I was put between two experienced mechanics. I had experience on both sides of me, but now I needed tools. I bought a small tool box which just wasn't sufficient for my job needs. I didn't have nearly enough tools, so I started buying tools like women buy groceries. Every week I bought new tools. At one time in my mechanical career, if they asked me for a certain wrench, I could say if they made two of them, I have one. I bought a much larger tool box and everything, I was straight rolling. Working there we didn't work overtime, just half days on Saturday. We worked five and a half days a week. We started and ended work at the same time everyday. Now I needed to make some money. I was making good money, but I needed to make more.

I went down to an Exxon Service Station, and talked to a guy there, I told him where I worked and the type work I was doing. He let me come to work there on my off time. He would save jobs for me. He gave me 60% of what I made. In the evening when I got off work, he would have several jobs lined up for me. I would do several sets of brake shoes, U-joints, wheel bearings, alternators, generators and starters. He would tell his customers that he had a man coming in at 5:30 if they wanted to bring their car back. With his help I built up a real good clientele. During the time I was working both jobs, I only went home to sleep.

I made enough with that job to pay my bills, so I was able to save my regular check. Detroit was much better to me than the other places where I had been. I lived on the East side with my sister at first then I moved to the West side in my own apartment. I didn't have any problems in Detroit. I stayed in Detroit and worked until I got drafted. Finally that draft board caught up with me, I got drafted!

I'M IN THE ARMY NOW

BY THE TIME I got drafted I was 26 years old. They gave me time to come back to Arkansas and when I was notified of the draft I got it transferred so I could report in at Little Rock, Arkansas. We got to Little Rock late one evening and they flew me and a whole lot of other young men from Little Rock to Fort Bliss, Texas.

⌒

I didn't have any real bad experiences in the military. Except one day when we were in basic training I ran into a young man from South Carolina and he had the same attitude as most of the people I had encountered back in Arkansas. This particular day we were doing what you call a 3-point landing. You have a baronet at the end of the rifle, you jump in this hole, they have a dummy in the hole, and you land with your feet and stick the rifle in the dummy. We had this young man from Alabama or Georgia, he was a young Black man, but he was very uncoordinated. The drill sergeant kept making him repeat the drill and try to make him do the 3-point landing right. The first time he punched himself in the chest with the butt of the rifle, the next time he had the rifle too far to the side when he had to drawback and stick the dummy, which just didn't work. This young man from South Carolina mouthed off to the drill sergeant, the exact words he said were, "Sergeant, you know he can't do that as good as we can, he's a nigger".

The young man that was in the hole crawled up out of the hole, looked at this guy, dropped his rifle and ran straight into him. He couldn't do a 3-point landing, but he could fight real well. He ran straight into him, on contact one arm went around the guy and his fist went directly in his face. He did *that* 3-point landing perfect. He hit that guy dead in the face. The boy went down and he went down on top of him and the sergeant took a walk. They fought around in the sand for five or six minutes. After a few minutes of them rolling and tumbling, the sergeant broke up the fight he formed us up and made those two, double time around us. After they double timed around us, he then put them down in front. He then took them out and made them do push-ups and then fall in the rear. We marched down the road a little ways, and then they trucked us in for chow. We went through the monkey bars and had chow, formed back up on the trucks and back down to the range again. We continued that until everyone got it right. It was hot, sandy, and windy--- so anyway, by the end of that day that boy was doing a 3-point landing as good as anybody. After that everyone got along just fine.

After basic I had a little time to come home, and then I reported to Fort Belvard, Virginia.

That was a good experience. I was from the country. I toured around the Capitol, Washington, D. C. and all the sights that were in that area. It was a good experience for me.

After that I got my orders to Viet Nam. I went by way of Anchorage, Alaska. I landed in Viet Nam Cameron Bay and from there was sent to an out post. I was a replacement soldier for an artillery unit. Since I didn't have any prior training in artillery, they made me a gun bunny. My job was to get the shell from the pit to the gun. After a year, I was back in the states.

I went back to Detroit and picked up where I left off, two years had passed. I went back to work at the car dealership, but not at the service station. I went to work at another service station closer to my house and I did the same thing all over again. I worked at the dealership by day and the service station in the evening and at night.

RETURN TO ARKANSAS

WELL, FIVE YEARS later after working and saving, I decided it was time to return to Arkansas. Before I got back to Arkansas I needed some land, so I bought two acres of land off the main highway. The land was about a mile off the main road. I had cleaned up a place to put my house and I moved over about a city block and cleaned up another place to build a shop; an auto mechanic shop, where I was going to work on cars.

The gentleman I bought the land from, Mr. Burnside, came through there one day and he stopped and asked, "What are you doing down here"? I told him I intended to work on cars and that I was cleaning a place to build my shop. He said, "You ought to go and talk to my sister, O'rell; she has some land up there beside the highway. She has a little piece on one side of the highway and a big piece on the other. I'm sure she will sell you that little piece that sticks out on the other side of Highway 82. You'd be much better off building your shop up there beside the highway. You will be easier to get to and you will have more customers." I said," okay." He told me that his sister had an office uptown, she was an attorney, and to talk with her and see if she wanted to sell me that little piece of land that's on the wrong side of the road.

Well it was on the main highway. I thought about it over the weekend and decided that it was a good idea. I got my dad to go with me to talk to this lady, this was in 1970. We went up to her office to talk with her. I had already told my dad how bad

I wanted this piece of land so whatever I had to pay for it, I was willing to pay.

We went to her office and as we came in she looked up at us. She didn't have a receptionist type of set-up. You just walked in the office and there she was. She looked up at us and said, "What do you 'boys' want?" I hesitated, but my daddy spoke. He said, "Ma'am, we came to talk to you about that little piece of land you have down beside the highway on the left side of 82 Highway. I want to know if you would sell it, we would like to buy that piece of land." She looked up at us and said, "No, you all just turn around and get on out of here." We started out, but my dad spoke again and said, "Ma'am, we would be willing to pay you a good price." She said, "But I don't want to sell it, you hear. I done told you that, so you all just get on out of here and stop bothering me. I have work to do." My dad took one step and said, "Well, would you take $200?" She said, "You ain't gonna want to pay enough." It was my money but my dad was fronting for me, so I was a little bit hesitant to jump in because I didn't want to say the wrong thing. Because when you were dealing with those older White women and you said one thing wrong, then you didn't have enough money to buy anything from them. My dad said, "We would be willing to pay as much as $500." She said, "That's not enough for the paperwork I've got to do, that's just not enough."

I had just bought two acres from that same family and paid $200 an acre. He had just offered her $500 for just a little over a quarter of an acre. But it was like a slice of pie, deep on one end and running out to nothing on the other end. We were willing to pay $500 for that little piece of land and she said, "No, I still don't want to sell."

He made it to the door and said, "Well we can scrap up as much as $600 if that's what it will take." She said, "You want that land awful bad for that 'boy'. That's who you want it for, don't you? You want it for that 'boy'," He said, "Yes ma'am." She said, "Well I still don't want to sell." My dad said, "Well before

I go let me go ahead and go as high as I can go. We'll go on and pay you $800 for that little piece of land." She said, "You really want that boy to have that land awful bad." He said, "Yes ma'am I do." She said, "If you want him to have it that bad, I'm gonna sell it to you. I will sell you that little ole piece of land for $800, if you can get $800." Well my dad had the money in his pocket right then. I had worked and saved for five years to do this thing, so $800 wasn't going to stop me. She said, "You can come back up here in about a week and I'll have the paperwork ready for you to sign. Now you will have to carry it to the courthouse and get it recorded and notarized." Then she said, "But I don't want no bunch of mess down beside that road. I own that land on the other side and I don't want no bunch of junk all up and down that road." My dad said, "Well he'll keep it pretty clean." She said, "You sure believe in that boy." I was a grown man, but to her all Black men were boys, and a young Black man was definitely a "boy".

I was so glad I carried my dad with me, because he just made everything work out fine. I'm sure I would have said, looked or done something to irritate her. She probably never would have sold that little piece of land to me alone.

We waited for a week. That week seemed like a whole year. I was anxious to get this land. We went back a week later. We waited until about 10:30 in the morning because he didn't want to go too early. He didn't want to be standing there when she got to the office. We went on up to her office and sure enough; she had all the paper work done. He gave her the $800 and we went to the courthouse and got it recorded and everything and that's how I got the first piece of land beside Highway 82.

I took the original two acres I had bought on the side road and bought a house and had it moved and gave that house to my mama and my daddy. They were still living on the original farm we grew up on and there was no electricity in their house. The road was still very bad. The road grader didn't work on the road, so it was rough getting in and out in wet weather. It was

45

2-1/2 miles back in to the farm and the creek was still there with no bridge. So I got my dad to agree that he and Mom would move into the house which I had moved onto the property. They had an indoor bathroom so my mama was real happy. Then I went to work at getting me a house built up on the highway property and building my shop. Since I was going to be on the main road, I decided to build a service station instead of just a mechanic shop.

I went to the block company and priced the material which would be needed to build the station. I got a man with a dozer to come out and clear the land. We got the driveways put in so the truck could deliver the blocks. We got the concrete poured for the floor, got the blocks laid and put on the top. I now had my building for my station. I then went to the Exxon Gas Company about getting gas pumps and gas for the station. I had a little money so everything was going smoothly.

After I got my service station opened I put the word out that I was interested in building a house. One of the guys that built houses got in touch with me. Well, what I did was have three different people dealing with me on building my house. I got a price and blueprint from one company, then another, and the other company. I then started playing two ends against the middle. I told one company what the other company could build my house for and asked them if they could beat that price. They told me they thought they could and I repeated this until I got the best price and I think I did pretty good. By the time I had selected a builder, I had saved $12,000 from the original bid. I then got my house built.

In the meantime, this lady that my daddy had bought the quarter acre of land from had told her brother that if she ever sold any more land she was going to sell it to me, because anybody that wanted land that bad and would pay that kind of money for a little ole piece of land, she wanted them to have the rest. The main body of the property was on the other side of the highway. It was a 40 acre tract, just short of the highway right-of-way.

46

When she died her brother came to my service station to fill up with gas one Monday morning. He said, "My sister passed – the one you bought this piece of property from – she passed over the weekend, and I'm going to tell you right now that she said that if any of her land was going to be sold she wanted it to be sold to you. She said any darky, (he was a little more of a friend) that wanted land as bad as you, deserved the opportunity to buy. She didn't have any children and I'm her brother and I'm going to inherit all this stuff. Now if you want it, I'll make sure you get the land." I told him right then, "Mister, I want the land." He said, "Okay, if you want it, I'll make sure you get the land. I won't advertise it; we will just have a quiet sale. It will just be you, me and the lawyer." That's how I got the forty acre across the highway from my shop.

Now why would I leave Detroit and come back to Arkansas? Well let me tell you about this little incident. I was working at the car dealership and my bay was right next to the service manger's desk. One day there was a White lady who brought her car in for a minor repair. The service manager told her, "You can wait while we make this minor adjustment, you won't have to wait very long". While she was waiting, there were three Black men who came in and each one of them was driving a brand new Lincoln. As soon as they went into the waiting room she lit into the service manager. She was chewing him up one side and down another. She had tried to buy a new car, I'll say a month earlier and she was turned down. She was really giving the service manager a hard time. I was working, but I was also listening.

She could not understand, or believe, these three Black men had brand new cars and she, being a White woman had been turned down. While I was in Detroit I encountered, not as often, but the same things I had encountered all my life living in the South and in Dallas. I had encountered the same hostility from White people in Detroit, not as often, but the same type of meanness.

Being Black and being raised in the South, I was highly trained in recognizing prejudice. White people seem to forget that Black people know how to recognize prejudice; they are trained by White people. They taught me how to see hostility.

Simple things like body language, the way you say good morning, the way you look at me; all are indications of the person that you are. You can talk to a lot of people and they might say, "I'm not prejudiced", but people forget that what they do speaks so loud that people most often don't hear what they say. When you say good morning to me, I read your tone of voice, the way you look at me, your body language; they all tell me a lot about you. So most Black people are good at recognizing prejudice.

Now this service station that I build was pretty nice. It had a hydraulic lift in one bay and a second bay to work in, a nice office with cash register. It had aluminum and glass roll up doors. It had a canopy to cover the pumps, so you could pump gas without getting wet by the rain.

I was repeatedly asked by White people who were not locals, "Boy where is the boss?" I would always read a certain tone of voice or a certain language in their quest to find out who owned the place. A lot of them once they realize I owned the place, would still stop again, but in a lot of cases when they found out I owned the place, instantly they were ready to go. Whatever they were selling or whatever they were peddling, they were through with me. But for every time there was a bad one, there would be five or six good ones. On an overall basis, once my station was up and running, the White people were good to me. The ones that were good were very good and the ones that were not, they kept moving. They didn't meddle or make trouble in any way, they just kept going. But the ones who supported me would stop by and we'd talk about grandkids, their kids or how the crops were growing. That I didn't mind, the hostile ones just left me alone and that was good.

A SEASON FOR ALL THINGS

I GREW UP as a young child remembering my Mama always telling us kids that when she was growing up she never had a store bought doll. Her mother made them what you call rag dolls. She would take some material and cut it out, then take a stick and stuff cotton into it and stuff the doll and sew up the hole where they stuffed in the cotton. Then they would take buttons and sew them on to make the eyes and nose. It was pretty nice, but she never had any store bought toys. So what I did, when I got older I went to the store one day and bought my mama five dolls, pretty dolls. I brought them home and gave them to her. After I gave her the five dolls, everybody laughed at me for buying my mama dolls. My mama took one of the biggest dolls and put it on the bed; we now had a guest room, now that all the kids were grown and gone. She had this room so when out of town company came they had a room of their own to sleep. She had a big, pretty bed in this room and she placed this doll up in the middle of that bed. The rest of them, over a period of time, she gave to grandkids; but she kept that one.

The lesson that I learned was those dolls didn't mean anything to her at that stage and time in life. She had grown past that. So I took that lesson and I went out and bought me some things that I never had as a child growing up--- a bicycle, a yellow bicycle, I bought a BB gun and some wind-up cars. Well, those things didn't mean anything to me either. I ended up giving them to my nephews. I still have the bicycle. I guess I've had that bicycle for over 40 years.

I learned a valuable lesson from that. At the time and point in life when things are important to you to acquire, if there's any way you can get them and stay between the two laws, the law of God and the law of man, then by all means you should. For whatever stage of life you are in, it's only for a season and when that season is over, they are like the leaves on the trees – they are only there for a season. When the time is out, it's only there for a season. Whatever you can get or enjoy for that season, you need to do it, because later on it won't mean anything to you. I have a lot of things I've done and places I've seen. I've been down into Old Mexico, I've been up to Canada, I've been to Viet Nam, I've been to Germany, I've traveled throughout the United States, but that was when I was in that season. I'm out of that season now; I don't jump at the idea of getting in a car and going on the highway for two weeks at a time. Short trips are about all I want to take now. My knees hurt, my back hurt, I get tired and I get sleepy and I don't really enjoy being on the road anymore. I go when I have to go and I go where I need to go, but the idea of getting in a car heading back to Detroit doesn't sound exciting to me anymore. So whatever it is you can do or whatever it is you want to do, if you are in that season, go ahead live life to the highest.

That brings up something else too, friends and associates, you know they come and they go. The idea of someone being your friend for life, when you are young chances are they are only there for a season and when that season is over they will move on or you will move on also. I think only the rocks last forever. Stay between the two laws, the law of God and the laws of man and enjoy what you can while you can, because when that season is over it won't mean anything to you later.

Life is a one way street. There is no going back when you pass a stage in life. All the good times you had as a child, as a teenager, once you pass that age, you can't reproduce those feelings. The people that were there and the state of mind they were in at that time, it's all passed.

Early in our marriage, my wife worked. When our children were young my wife went to work everyday. She worked and saved right along with me. So whatever we accomplished, we did it together. She doesn't work now, but when I buy something, I still know that I'm spending our money. It's not just mine because I'm the only one working now. We worked and saved and invested together and that's how we got to where we are now.

~

I was surprised that I would have a son-in-law that I really admire, but I really respect my son-in-law. He is a fine young man. He takes good care of my daughter and my three grandkids, so you know how much I care for him. I'm so proud of him. I tease my daughter a lot. I told her, "You went out and found a young man I liked." He's eager to learn and he doesn't feel like he knows everything. I can read that when I give him instruction he appreciates, rather than thinking, "This old man is trying to boss me." We don't agree on everything, but he's educated enough to know that if I disagree with him I'm not fighting him, but we have a difference of opinions. He's not a big man, but he's big in heart and big in spirit, and the young man goes to church. So we can talk about what the preacher preached about. So my daughter did real well.

My wife is a musician. She can play the piano and organ. She is also a seamstress. My mother would have been proud of her, because she can really make a rag doll. She also teaches piano lessons. Once a year she has a recital and then she gives her students and their family a Fun Day at our home. We fish and I give a tour of the farm and tell them about the cows and trees and nature. We cook and eat and just have a great day.

My daughter-in-law is studying to be a veterinarian. She is very beautiful and she is kind and sweet. She loves the farm and all animals. If she could she would adopt every stray animal there was in the world. My son did equally as well as my daughter in picking a keeper. But one thing is missing – the grand kids. When she finishes school we want some new additions to that family. She is truly a jewel and a welcome addition to our loving family. The most remarkable thing about both my son-in-law, Reggie, and my daughter-in-law, Miriam, they are both from South Arkansas. Both my son and daughter attended out of state colleges and it's amazing they would meet home folks, to marry.

I can say I've lived in two different South Arkansas' from the 40's, 50's, 60's, 70's, 80's, and 90's and up until the present time. Up until about the 80's South Arkansas was very different from what it is now. Up until around the 80's there was enough prejudice around South Arkansas to oppress most of the average Black people. But I would say from the 80's, South Arkansas has made a complete turn around. I can only speak for South Arkansas. I can't speak for the rest of the world. Now it's a different South Arkansas from what it was back when I was younger. Now in South Arkansas you can go anywhere you want, you can live anywhere you, and you can have anything that you can afford.

I'd like to again mention this gentleman, Mr. Pratt, who when I bought my first two cows, let me use his trailer to haul my cows to his farm to get them bred. He had some sons and they are good friends of mine. Those three brothers treat me like a Black brother. I can go to any of their houses and they invite me in the front door. No, I don't go to their house sitting around trying to wear their furniture out, but I don't visit a lot of Black people either and sit around wearing out their furniture. Anything they can help me with, anything I need, any type of advice or any kind of equipment I need, all I have to do is make a phone call. If I don't have time to go and get it, I can look up and one of them is bringing it to me. So it's a better situation now. It's an area where a long time ago the license plate read, "Land of Opportunity." I can say in the last 20 to 25 years the people of South Arkansas have been trying to live up to that name. No we don't have an abundance of high paying jobs in this area. We make comfortable livings in this area. And yes, there are still some prejudiced people, but I just think there has always been and there will always be prejudiced people. But the good now outnumber the bad and that's basically all you can expect.

BETTER SOUTH ARKANSAS

THINGS IN SOUTH Arkansas are so much better now than they were when I was a boy in the 1940's. Let's look at some of the situations I had to encounter. When I was a boy I would go to the store with my daddy. My mother would write out a grocery list of things she needed him to bring back from the store. We would go to the store and my dad would give the store keeper the grocery list. Then this man would go from aisle to aisle in the store gathering up the supplies that was on her list. They would put the items on the counter. He would begin to add up the goods and a White person would come in and he would stop what he was doing to wait on the White people. He would just simply rake my dad's stuff aside. He would wait on them and we would just have to stand around and wait. They would talk about school, the children, grandchildren and farming. He would get through checking them out and he would go back to my dad's groceries. In the middle of finishing up my Dad's order, in would come another White person. If it was a woman, he would say, "Ma'am, can I help you?" When he finished with her he would start on Dad's items again. I have been in the store with my dad to get items and we would have to wait on him to wait on three or four people before he would finish my dad's order.

We don't have to do that anymore. We go in the store and get what we want and wait in line. Whoever is next gets waited on next. The banks would do you the same way. You could be in line taking care of your business and they would excuse themselves from you if a White person came in and start working with them. Even if they had to fill out papers, you would just have to wait. When they finished with them, then they would come back and complete your business.

I know you're thinking, "I would just go somewhere else." But where else could you go? Everyone was the same and there was only one bank and one or two stores in town. So you had to accept whatever treatment they issued. When they totaled your bill you didn't question it, because if you did you might offend him, the store owner, and he would then tell you to "Go to another store 'Boy', you don't question me." If you decided to go to the next store, he had already sent him word that you were a smart one and you thought you could out count him. So it wasn't a good situation. We were more or less at their mercy.

It was the same experience at the cotton gin. We raised a few bales of cotton every year. When you got to the cotton gin and they were unloading your cotton, and there was a White man behind you, he would just tell you, "I need to go on and get Mr. Sam's cotton because he has a long way to go," or "He's going to try and get another load today so I need to go on and get him out." So you had to wait and there was nothing you could do about it, but just wait.

Back in the 50's and 60's there were a lot of gravel roads. The main highway was paved, but just about all the side roads were gravel. Now there was no law that said you couldn't pass a White man on a dirt road, except *his* law. That was something you just didn't do. If he was in front of you, you did not pass him. I remember riding with my dad, and a White man would pass us, now they could pass you, and my dad would pull over to the side of the road and wait until the dust cleared and then he would continue driving. Then sometime he would just slow down extra slow and let the dust settle. Because in the summertime we on the average would get one or two rains in June and it might rain once or twice in July and sometime in the month of August you would only get a shower, all those dirt roads would turn to powder. You'd drive down the road and all the trees and everything on the side of the road would be just covered in dirt. That's how dusty the roads would get in the summer. But of course there was not as many cars back then as there are today, so the traffic wasn't real bad.

Back then *any* White man you talked to was "Yes Sir or No Sir" and he was "Mister." I don't care who he was or where he was from. And you were "Boy" and if he didn't refer to you as *Boy*, and you were old, I mean really old, they called you "Uncle". If it was an older Black lady, she would be "Auntie". If they were talking about you and your name was Tom, you would not be Tom; you would be "Old Tom". That was like an unwritten thing that they all did. That was a way you could distinguish in their conversation the race of the person they were talking about. If they were talking about a Black person, he would be "Old Tom". But if they were talking about a White person they would say, "Last week me and Tom went on a fishing trip."

So you see what I'm talking about. I have gone from *Boy to Old Mack* and now I'm referred to as *Mr. Mack*. I stop at a local store now and the store owner and all his workers greet me, "Good morning Mr. Mack, Mr. Mack would there be anything else for you?" So when I tell you that I've lived in two different South Arkansas' that's what I'm talking about. As a young man all I was referred to was Old Mack, "I'm going to get Old Mack to do this", "If you see Old Mack out back, tell him I said come in here". If I wasn't referred to as Old Mack, I was referred to as Boy. "If you see that boy out there, tell him I need him to do such and such". We had a handle before our name, but it was not a handle of respect.

Now days even the guys I work with, I work with a fine bunch of White men, we can be sitting outside and one of them will get up to get a cup of coffee and will actually bring me a cup. They will ask, "What do you want sugar, cream or black"? Now I can remember the days when you could have taken anyone of those White men and beat them with a stick and they would have still refused to bring me a cup of coffee. There was no way they would have given a Black man a cup of coffee. But now they will even share food off their plate with me and even eat food out of my lunch box.

It is a very big difference from when I worked out back at the wash rack. I know I have to leave all this. I worked a lot of years and a long time to get to this point. Now I want to stay around a little while longer to kind of enjoy where I worked so hard to get. *To work on a job and be treated as an equal---quite an achievement.*

There is a company that comes in my plant and does a recovery service for us. Usually each time they come in the plant, I get assigned to work with these people. This company has offered to hire me several times, but some people don't realize when they are successful. I get what I need from where I work and I am perfectly and totally satisfied working where I am. I work with a great bunch of people who appear to appreciate what I do. It took me a very long time to reach this work status. Happiness and satisfaction at this time in life is more important than more money. So I'll stay put.

Now I've told you a lot of things about the places I've been and the struggles I have had, but here is what I see now. Eight out of ten White men have already taken their foot off the necks of Black men. No longer do we work on jobs doing the same work with different pay. Things are better, times have changed. Opportunities are out there, but what I see is Black people out of jealousy, or lack of commitment is still being left behind.

AT THE STORE

MY MAMA AND my sisters would not buy any underclothes at the local stores. They didn't like the way the store owners would display the underclothes. They would place the items in front of them to determine if they would fit. They didn't like that so they never would buy any underclothes locally. They would get them from mail order catalogs. There was a company that sent out catalogs and you could pick out what you wanted. You would fill out an order blank and order by mail because the folks in the stores would hold the items in front of you and if you let them do that and made a purchase, the next time you came into the store, they would ask you did they fit or how did they fit in front of other people. My mama and sisters though that was very disrespectful, so they would never buy their underclothes locally.

Of course, there was no such thing as trying on a dress in the local store. You could hold a dress up in front of you and see if it fit, but there was no such thing for them to go into a store and try on a dress, skirt or blouse. You could try it on when you got home, if it was too tight you could take it back, but if it was to large you just had to make it work. If it was a little too long, you just put in another hem. They were not allowed to try on a dress in the store. Of course it was a situation where my mama didn't take all of us kids to the store to buy shoes either. She would take a piece of cardboard, put it down on the floor and you put your foot on top of the card board. She would then trace the shape of your foot onto the cardboard. They would take that to town and that's how they bought our shoes, by matching the card board to the right sized shoe. Most of the time they would be right, but sometime they would be too tight and you would put a piece of towel of something on the floor and try the shoe on after you got it home. They wanted to make sure you didn't put scuff marks on that sole, because if it didn't fit, you couldn't return a scratched shoe to the store. You would have to give a scuffed shoe to another one of your children with a smaller foot. If it was a little too big, they would pack some cotton in the toe of the shoe so it wouldn't be too loose on your foot. They had a way of doing things. It may sound a little corny now, but it worked for us back then.

Sometimes somebody from town would have extra clothes and shoes. They would put them in a sack and send them to us. People were good about sharing back then. You didn't have garage sales; they just passed the abundance and not needed items on to someone who needed them. If they had some good shoes that their kids had outgrown, they would send them to the country. So if you got a pair of nice shoes that someone sent, you didn't send them back. If they weren't just too awful tight, you could take and pack those shoes full of cotton seeds. Take them, sit them on the floor and pack them slam full of cotton seeds. Then you would pour water into the shoe onto the cotton seed, fill the shoe with water and as the cotton seed would swell, they would stretch the shoe. Now if it was too short, now that was different. There wasn't much you could do with it, but if it was just too tight on your feet, then the cotton seed procedure would work just fine. When water was applied, the cotton seeds would swell up and stretch the leather. The next day when you would try the shoes on again, if it felt pretty good you could go ahead and wear the shoes. But there were a lot of kids who grew up wearing shoes too big and too small. If you wore shoes that were too little, they would make corns on your toes and callous on your feet, but all and all, we still survived.

I never went to a barber shop until I was about 17 years old. My mama ordered some clippers from that mail order catalog. You worked them by hand. We didn't have electricity, so they were hand powered. She had a good pair of scissors, so she cut our hair herself. We never got a hair cut from a barber until we were old enough to work and pay for our own. It wasn't a situation where Mama didn't want us to have a barber shop haircut; it was just the fact that with so many of us kids and only one man working, they couldn't afford to send us boys to the barbershop to get a haircut. She would sit in a chair; we would sit on the floor. She would get the comb, clippers and the scissors. She would give us a haircut every couple of weeks. It didn't look as good as a barbershop cut, no where near, but that's what I had to wear until I was about 17 years old. I remember I couldn't wait until I could afford to get a haircut from a professional barber. That was one of my first goals--- as soon as I got a job and went to work I was going to a real barber. I know that sounds kind of square right now, but that was a big hill to climb for me--- to go to the barbershop and get a real haircut.

You know I've heard it said a lot of times that children who were abused or neglected during their childhood are most likely to abuse and neglect their own children. I don't know about all that, but I know I never wanted my children to have to go through the things that I had to endure in life. I always wanted bigger and better things for my children. That's why I would sit and talk to them about how to stay within the law, the value of saving, love, kindness and understanding for other people. Because I never wanted them or their children to ever have to go through the things I had to go through as a child. I know children can be very cruel to other children. It's not everybody who teaches their children love, kindness and understanding and the fact that everyone has a right to exist no matter how different they may be physically. Children will tease and pick at other children about their shoes, clothes, and yes, even hair. I, as a boy coming up, was often teased about my shoes, my clothes and yes, my haircut.

It was a situation where you've heard it said, that *you're damned if you do and damned if you don't*. Well either I needed a haircut or had just gotten a haircut. If I didn't get a haircut, then my hair would grow long and woolly. I have extremely course, in other words, nappy hair. If I told Mama I didn't want a haircut this week, it would get long and shaggy and did not look good. So I would get teased because I needed a hair cut. If she cut it, I would get teased because I had a jacked-up haircut. Because when you cut with hand clippers and scissors, there was no line, no shape, uneven cuts and it really did look rough. But I endured things of that nature as a child and I never wanted my children to have to experience that type of embarrassment.

I have touched on a lot of things in this book. As harsh as some of it may seem, it is all real. However, I never want to dwell on the negative. They are only in this book to point to the positive. I want to emphasize on some instructional advice. I hope my experiences show that it is just good to do good, persistence will pay off, and just because you have struggles in life doesn't mean you won't succeed in life. I hope I showed someone how you can take your weak points and turn them into strong points. I tried to show the value of love and understanding. I did all of these things and told you about all of these things to let you see how life was in South Arkansas for an ordinary rural black boy.

I think that all of my adversity and rejection made me work that much harder to succeed. I had to channel all of the negatives into positive, move forward energy. I was already out back; I couldn't afford to stay in that position. I had to work hard because if my family was going to ever enjoy the dreams I had for them; it was going to come from my hard work and determination.

I had to become conscientious of my habits, improve my saving techniques to turn a bad situation around. I had to learn the lesson of sacrifice. I said earlier that any man who makes enough to live makes enough to save; even if you have to put quarters in a jug. Just keep on doing that and eventually you will need another jug.

It is important that we be good stewards of our finances. If you make top money and you are living from pay check to pay check, then you need to change your spending habits. There is a problem. I said earlier that if you don't grow you have a problem. The same can be said for your savings. It is not the big pile, but the constant input that adds up in the long run. If you never sacrifice and save then you will never have any savings. You can't keep spending year after year and expect things to change; you must change your spending habits. It takes time to accumulate, even in the best of conditions, but most definitely when you come from an under privileged background as myself and others.

It is most important that we take advantage of every opportunity. When I grew up the opportunities were not there for people of color, that's just facts. But thanks to time and many changes, we are basically at the same level of opportunity. But too many of our young people are not prepared for the job of living in these times. I hear so many young people say, "I'm a quick learner. I can learn to do anything." But they fail to learn when they should---in school. The work force is not really your learning field, it is for trained workers. Why should an employer hire a trainee when there is a full pool of trained workers applying for a job? Get your education---in school, college and trade schools. Have something to offer an employer besides just a trainee.

I am a licensed fork truck operator, licensed crain operator and licensed mechanic. I am also a welder. I took my time to learn these things, so I would have something to offer an employer. You must sacrifice the time to be trained and then you can take advantage of all the opportunities this land offers.

I was in the active military service for two years and twenty years in the Army National Guard. In that period of time I met and was associated with a lot of men and basically all of them wanted the same things, a decent job and decent pay so they could support their families and give them the things they needed in life. All things are within reach, with self determination and hard work, they are obtainable.

If I could call Dr. Martin Luther King, Jr. back and let him have a look of South Arkansas, he would be very proud of where we've come from and where we are today, for this is truly, truly a land of opportunity.

You know in a storm a lot of your big trees will blow over. They are so rigid they won't bend, while that little tree that's standing underneath the big one will survive the storm because it will bend and not blow over. So just because you don't have today doesn't mean you will never have; and just because you do have, it doesn't mean you will always have; because storms will come.

You know they say behind every good man is a good woman. In my case that's true. Look through me and you will see my wife standing behind me telling me to "go on, write this book if that's what you want to do. Go on and reach for your goals and anyway I can help you, I will". Just look through me and you will see her standing there. Look through me and you will see my mother on a cold rainy night sitting by the heater, reading the bible to entertain the family. Look through me and you will see my father sitting over in a corner telling me, "Son, if you are ever going to have anything, you can't be starting out fresh every Monday morning." Look through me and you will see those strong people standing behind me, telling me to go ahead and do what you have to do. Just look through me.

YOUR WORD IS YOUR BOND

BACK AT THE well service, the man that I worked directly under was Mr. Bud Welch. Some times the other men would get to teasing me or riding me about something, Mr. "B" would have to walk the tight rope. He had to get them off of me, but not antagonize them, not let it seem as if he was directly taking up for me. He would say something like "ya'll get on out of here and leave that boy along, that boy's got work to do. Ya'll ain't got nothing to do. Go on out to the store because he's got work to do, ya'll leave him alone." He knew what he was doing. He would take up for me to get them off me, but he didn't want to do it directly because back in those days white people had a name for white people who took up for black people. They wouldn't call him that name to his face, but they would call him that behind his back and he knew, so he didn't want to antagonize them when he would get them off me. Neither did he want to come on too strong as though he was taking up for me. I know what you are thinking. *Why didn't I take up for myself?* Well, when you had one young black man and five or six white men, the more you pushed back the more they would push on you. So I would just look to him to get them off me.

Mr. "B" was a very strong man. He was a man who was going to do what he said he would do if it caused him money. I saw him make deals with other men and seal them with just a handshake. That handshake and nod of the head was better than any contract you could write. If he said he was going to do something, you could take it to the bank. He used to tell me, "Your word is your bond. I'm doing what I said I'd do. If you say it, then do it."

THE FARM

THERE WAS A man who had a farm; Mr. Mack Pratt. Not a very big man but a real mild mannered man. He had this farm and there were about 6 or 7 families who lived on his farm. He provided them with a basic house---a front porch, living room, bedroom, kitchen and an outhouse. I never knew him to cuss or dog anybody. He was always concerned about the old people in the community. He raised potatoes, corn, sorghum, ribbon cane and he usually raised a big garden also, out back of his house—about a 2 acre garden where he raised food products. He paid his workers $2 a day. During the spring when there was a lot of work on the farm, plowing and planting, pulling potatoes slips and bundling them up, getting ready to go to the field. His philosophy was, "If I have to watch you work, I don't need you." We would always gather out back under the shade trees and he would come out and send so many people to do this and so many to do that and in most cases he would go back into the house until about mid morning. But he was not going to stand around and watch you. If he did come out an: caught you under the shade tree he would come over and talk with you. He didn't want you to jump up and run back to work. If you were sitting down when he came up he just wanted you to keep sitting and talk with him. He would say, "I'm not worried about how much you've done when I get here, I just want to see what you've done at the end of the work day." He lived by that principle. He provided for the countryside in a five mile radius of where he lived. He provided people with a job.

The thing that I remember most about him was in the fall when the crops were gathered, all the potatoes dug, the corn pulled, the cotton picked, the sorghum and cane processed into syrup, he would always work it out to where all the workers would come for that one last day to clean up and put up tools and get things put away for the winter. Somehow we would always get through with most of that stuff around lunch time. Then he would go to the store and buy about $5 worth of bologna, another $5 worth of pressed ham, a jar of sandwich spread – the kind with pickles, a jar of mustard, a pound of hook cheese, 5 pounds of sugar and about 5 or 6 packages of red Kool-Aid and bread. He would let everyone out back eat bologna or pressed ham sandwiches then he would pay everybody. He even paid us for that day when we had the end of season picnic.

I often think about those days. The company I work for now does basically the same thing that he did way back then. We call them company picnics, the same thing, or we have a major shut down and after the shut down we buy steaks. They will pull a couple of guys off the job, to cook. We will all gather around the administration building and we get paid for that day. Today we have a new workforce, but basically the same theory.

Mr. Mack was a man that really cared about people in the community. He would ask when was the last time you saw Bruno. How is he doing, can he still get around? Older people that once worked for him and were not able to work anymore, he would say, "I want you all to go by there and take him a few bushels of potatoes, take him a few gallons of syrup, that was some good syrup we made this year." Whatever he had he was more than willing to share with the community. He provided a lot of people with jobs and he cared about the older people. When we were out in the hot fields chopping cotton, He would suggest to the older men, "Now look, I'm going to put you under the shade tree. I want you to sharpen hoes today." And perhaps to another older man he would suggest, "You take care of the water today." He was real concerned about the well fare of his workers. Our work force has lost that factor today. We lost that individual care. One thing about Mr. "M", his philosophy was that a man should give an honest days work for an honest days pay. He only paid $2 a day, but that was the going rate for field hands. $2 then was like $20 today.

Back in those days we were just field hands and dress codes didn't mean anything, but today it bothers me that our young people don't know how to dress or act on a job interview or job search. You do not wear night club clothes to an interview. You do not go to a construction job in a three-piece suit. Neither would you go to an office job interview in construction clothes and work boots. You must learn to present yourself appropriately because first impressions are forever. There is only one first impression and you must make that one good. You don't get a second chance. It really disturbs me about some of the attitudes our young people have. Pride is good, but keep it in its proper perspective. I hear so many young people say, "If they don't hire me the way I am, they just won't hire me. I mean, I'm just who I am, my hair, my clothes, whatever. If they want somebody they will hire me just like I am." Well, you forgot the Golden Rule --- He who has the gold makes the rules. You can't just walk in off the street and expect a major company to change their policy to accommodate you. If you need the job then you must make the adjustment to their rules. Pride can be your worst enemy misdirected. Remember that.

BELL COW

BACK YEARS AGO when I was a boy, my parents, uncles and aunts and most of the community had cows. Everybody's cows would run together as one herd. They would get together from all the small lots and pasture and go down into the back country and graze. I guess this was more open range. In the evening all the cows would get together and come home. But every cow, just like children, would go to their individual owner. Our cows would come to our home, my cousins' would go to their house and within that group of cows there was a lead cow. One of the owners would pick out the lead cow and would put a collar with a bell on the lead cow. When you went into the back country looking for the cows, you would listen for the bell. They also called her the "Bell cow". That cow determined when they would move, how long they would stay at a certain location and when they were coming back. All the cows followed her lead. When they were in the back country and the Bell cow was ready to go back into the community, she would "moo" and the other cows would hear her and they would come out of the back country and back to their individual homes. Now if those cows could follow the rules, why can't we? You will be left behind if you cannot follow the rules in the game of life.

My farm is a nice sized area and it has rolling hills so you can't visually see from one side to the other. So when the cows are asleep and the herd gets up and moves and one cow doesn't wake up and make the move, she will wake up later and find herself out there under a shade tree all by herself. She will get up and begin walking and looking, then she will begin to moo, to call the herd. When she is close enough so that the other cows can hear her, one of the cows will answer. Then she will go and link up with the herd. Now if cows can show compassion to one another, why can't we? The cow that was walking and moo-ing, we call a "Lost cow." Now why can't we show compassion for a lost friend or love one? Part of the intention of this book is to change your ways that may not be working for you. I know if cows know how to call out when they need help, we should. But most important is the herd that answers the call. We should also be understanding of someone's lost condition and want to help. I wonder why we can't be that considerate. I hope this book will help show you the way. In a herd of cows there are one or two older cows and the farmer calls these cows Auntie Cows. Because a lot of times a young heifer will have her first or second calf and cannot supply enough milk to feed her calf, then the auntie cows will share their milk with the young heifer's calf. Is this not showing love and compassion for one another? We are the intelligent beings, why can't we show love and kindness toward one another? We have become a cruel and evil society with not much kindness among us. We need to watch the cows and pull our society back together.

HONEY CAKES

IT WAS IN the late 50's or maybe in the late 60's, my mama used to make Honey Cakes. She would take and mix-up a cake like you would cook a sheet cake nowadays, but before she would cook it, she would pour honey in it, stir it up real good and pour it in a large bread pan. She would then put it inside the oven of the wood stove and bake this cake. As the stove heater was heating the house, it also served as the cook stove. Then when the kids would come home and go into the kitchen and wanted something to eat and dinner wasn't ready, she would just look on the table and cut them a piece of Honey Cake. It was good and sweet and had a honey flavor. It's the same thing as an afternoon snack that the mothers of today give, except they usually just give bought cookies or snacks. That was something really good.

If she didn't make a Honey Cake, she would make what we called Cracklin Bread. To make crackling bread, she would make up a batch of corn bread and add crackling (some pig skin). When they killed hogs they would take all the pig skins and fat meat, put it in an iron pot, build a fire and cook the grease out of the fat meat. They would save the cooked out skins and meats, and make crackling bread. If there was no crackling bread or honey cake, she would take a piece of cornbread, split it open and fill it with sugar syrup. To a hungry kid that was some good eating. That would hold you until she got dinner ready.

The grease that they cooked out from the pigskin and fat meat was called Lard. They would take that grease; put it in jars and gallon buckets. They would take it and put in a little building they called a fruit house. Back in those days, almost everybody in the country had a fruit house where they would keep all of their food supplies. Back in those days they would can all kinds of food. We didn't have the luxury of having a freezer so they used the canning method to preserve food. They would cook it, put it in jars sealed tight and turn those jars upside down, so they could cool and seal. Then they would put the jars of preserves in the fruit house. There was always something out in the fruit house to make a meal. They canned peaches, plums, blackberries, apples, pears and also meats. They would cook them down real low and get about 90% of the water out of them. They would put them in a jar, put a lid on, put them on the table and let it cool. The next day they would take that out to the fruit house. That was our canned goods department at the shopping center. When Mama would get ready to make dinner or supper in the evening, you would see her go out to the fruit house and come back with a few jars of something that she had canned last summer.

All of those old people had a way of making a life out of meager means. There wasn't much money back in those days, but there was a lot of knowledge of how to make life work, to get by and survive. I don't know how, I wonder sometime to this day just exactly how it was done, how did they survive. But with a house full of kids and one man working, there was always food on the table. Back in those days people prioritized things—they did what they knew they had to do to survive, and they were good at this.

During blackberry picking time you would get a couple of big buckets and you would take them to the field. When you got to the field, you would set the big bucket down and use a small bucket to pick the berries. When the small bucket was full, you would pour the berries into the big bucket. People reserved the edge of the fields for blackberries, plums and hackberries. Up near the house there would be a peach orchard. Their plum orchard would be maybe a half of a city block of nothing but plum trees. They didn't require much pruning or a lot of work. A lot of times you would be plowing in the fields and the plum trees were trying to grow out to the edge of the fields, you would actually plow some of them up, to keep them from spreading, and to keep the orchard from getting so big. Blackberries were the same way. The vines grew along the fence and you would take a stick and knock the undesirable vines out of your way so that you could get up into the vines to reach the best berries. They didn't require any maintenance—just go into the fields and pick blackberries.

We could pick all we needed and we could also sell some of them. They just grew naturally around the fields. We would gather blackberries. My mother would make blackberry pies, blackberry cobblers and blackberry jam. During the winter when blackberry season was over and Mama wanted to make a blackberry cobbler, she would just go out to the fruit house and get a couple jars of blackberries She did the same with peaches and all the other fruits. That was just a way of life.

The Lard that was cooked out from the pig fat, there would be some of it left over and we would save it until spring. If you tried to keep it too long, it would get old and it would get rank (develop a musty odor). They wouldn't throw it away either. They would take the left over lard from the last season and the old bones that they had carved all the meat off, put them in a wash pot, put some lye in there and start it to boiling and make what they called "Lye Soap". We could make the lye soap as good as you wanted. It was used for everything. We washed everything with it---your hands, your clothes and you could even bath with this soap. They would take the lye soap, let it cool after they cooked it down and would then checked to see if it was good soap. They would determine this by looking at the bubbles on top of the water as the mixture boiled. They could tell the quality of the soap by how it bubbled. They would allow it to cool and it would solidify. They would then take a knife and cut the soap into bars. They would then put it out in the smokehouse to dry. Once it was dried, it was as good as any soap you could buy in the store. It didn't have a scent, it had a lye soap smell, but it was good for cleaning everything.

During the winter we would put the cows and the horse in the fields to eat the left over grain. We had to buy a little bit of grain for additional feed. We raised a lot of the feed for our animals, but we still had to buy some. The feed would come in designer sacks, floral, strips and prints. These sacks were used to make blouses for the girls and shirts for the boys. You would see the old people looking through the feed sacks at the store because they wanted to get one like the one they had gotten last time, or because they didn't have quite enough material to finish that girl's dress or looking to make sure they didn't get one exactly like the last one because they didn't want to make two girl's dresses just alike. Today when you talk and think about these things you laugh, but that was the way of life back then.

During the first part of the summer when the peas in the fields would start to get ready, we would eat peas and bread. We would have a little meat to go with them, but we would eat peas and bread all week. There would be whole weeks when we ate peas and bread only. On Sunday we would have something different. We would have bread and peas with some meat. Peas and bread, bread and peas, anyway you say it, it's the same.

THE BANK ACCOUNT

THERE WAS A man I knew who worked at the local sawmill, where they rigged up some type of trolley to pull stacks of lumber from one place to the next. One day the cable broke and the backlash of the cable cut off his arm. The man got $10,000 for the loss of his arm and a lifetime job at the mill. After he got his $10,000 he talked so ugly, to the man running the mill and he adamantly didn't want his job back. He had $10,000. He was rich, he had plenty of money. He bought a car and there was a party at his house every weekend. His word was, "Come on boys, let's have some fun, the drinks are on me". In about six months the man was broke. He went to the bank and put his initials on a check and told the lady at the window that he wanted $100. The lady went to the book and came back and asked him if he wanted to close his account. He said, "No, he wanted $100." The lady told him he only had $27 in his account. That man acted up so badly at the bank that day, until they called the police. The police came and he still acted up, so they carried him to jail. The reason he was acting up so, was because he still had a lot of pages left in his check book. A lack of education and a lack of knowledge is a sad thing. Education is power. This poor man could not understand the concept of banking; he associated his bank book with his availability of money. Get an education.

≈

Now that it's getting on up into the summer, we've been on peas for awhile. Now corn and sweet potatoes are starting to get ready. In the potato patch when you looked at the ground along where the potatoes were growing, you would notice the ground cracking. It's now time to start digging potatoes. The potatoes would be dug up to check for proper sizes. If they were not big enough to put into your bucket, they would then be covered back up, so they could grow some more. The corn fields were also ready to be picked. Tending the corn, would give the peas time to continue growing and turning blue and then they would dry. We would go and pick the peas after they start drying. These peas would be for the winter. The dry peas would then be put in a cloth sack. Outside in the yard using a stick, the sack of peas would be whipped until the hull and peas separated. A bed sheet would be put on the ground, then taking a bucket—one of the bigger girls would stand and pour the peas from the bucket to the bed sheet. She would hold the bucket up real high while pouring the peas. In the meantime, another girl would be on the other side with a card board fanning the peas as they were being poured. The air would blow peels and husks away from the peas. Then the peas would be put in a sack and hung in the fruit house. That winter someone would go to the fruit house and get some dry peas, bring them in the house and put some water on them in a big dish pan. The good peas would sink and all the husks would come to the top of the water along with all the bad peas. The unwanted husk and hull would be skimmed off the top and all the good peas would be left at the bottom. We would take the husks and bad peas skimmed off the top, and throw them outside for the chickens. The chickens in the yard would come running because they had something to eat. You would take those dry peas and let them soak and then cook them and you'd have peas all over again.

Mama would some days take peas and over-cook them, cook most of the water out of them, and make pea biscuits. She would take the simmered peas, add some flour, chop some onions, add a little seasoning and make a batter. She would then pat this batter into pones and drop it in hot grease and fry them. It would be similar to a salmon patty. That would put food on the table and give us something a little different from what we had been eating everyday. That was some good eating. She would always cook more than she thought we could eat in one meal so there would always be leftovers for a hungry stranger.

Now summer was about over. We would go into the garden where the peas and other vegetables were planted.   It would take about three boys, some shovels and they would go out and turn the soil over. By jumping up on the shovel and pushing it down and flipping the dirt over, we would be getting ready to plant the fall turnips. In just a little while there would be turnips, up and ready to eat for the fall. After they made good sized roots, we would go out and pull the big roots and go to the corner of the garden and do what we called "bank them". This was done by placing the turnips roots on the ground in layers and then covering them with pine straw. The pine straw would hold the moisture. This process was completed by covering the pine straw with dirt.   The rest of the winter we would have good turnips they would keep and not get soft. We didn't have the green tops, but we had some mighty fine roots.

Back in those days, the church was the meeting place. After the preacher finished preaching and church was out, nobody wanted to leave the church. Everybody would sit around outside and talk and visit with each other, because it would maybe a couple of weeks or so before they would see each other again.

Church was the meeting place. Mama would talk to somebody; they might be running low on potatoes, or peanuts, or something. She would tell them, "I'll send my boys over there Tuesday with a sack of potatoes or something. We would get up Tuesday morning and Mama would have us get a sack of potatoes and take them clear across the bottom, over to a neighbor's house.   When we got over there, the person would insist on us eating something before we started back home. We would get there about mid morning. She would probably give one of us a bucket to go down to the spring to get some fresh water and she would say, "I'm going to make you boys some Kool-aid before you go". She'd give us Tea cakes or Ho cakes or something to eat before we left. Because of the conversation she had with our mother at church, she knew we were coming. That was one of the good things about the way people were back then.

In the late 50's we started to get modern. We had a good year on the farm, we sold a few bales of cotton, Daddy sold a few head of cows, and we bought us an ice box and a butane tank. Keep in mind now, we didn't have any electricity. It was a butane ice box. It would sit there and you would hear a little clicking noise, and underneath the ice box was a little blue flame. Blue fire would light up and make a little hissing sound until it cooled back down the ice. I don't understand to this day how that fire made ice, but it did. It had ice trays in the top of it. You would take the ice trays out, pour a little water over the back of the tray and the ice would slip right out. But later on, my dad bought some ice trays you didn't have to pour water on, you'd take it out and pull a little lever attached across the top and the ice would break loose and fall out. We had gotten uptown. We had really gotten to the top of the line. He wanted that butane tank to sit in the front yard so everybody who came by, could see we had a butane tank.

After another year or two he bought my mama a butane cook stove. That meant we didn't have to chop stove wood anymore!

Things started to get a little better. I guess you could say that after half the kids had grown up and moved on, things really got better. He finally had a man to come out and run an extra pipe from the stove over to the living room and bought her a butane heater. Of course the man had to bring the butane in the fall of the year, to make sure he got out there and put the butane in before the rainy season started, because once winter set in, the road would get so bad the truck couldn't get through. They would bring butane in the fall and it would have to last until the spring when the weather was better. Once or twice we ran out, spring didn't come as quickly as we needed. We were out of butane so we had to wait on the truck, but we survived.

I can remember nights when the clicking sounds would start and we would lie on the floor and be amazed at that blue fire under the ice box. I know you are probably laughing right now, but it was something that amazed us kids to lie on the floor and look at that blue flame.

We also had chickens, which served three purposes. One, we would always get fresh eggs, two, you could eat the meat and three; they were a form of pest control. They would keep the bugs, worms and insects under control because that's what they ate all day. So we weren't bothered with a lot of bugs and worms and ticks around the yard. Those chickens served a very good purpose.

Our dogs served three purposes also. They were our watch system. They would bark and alarm us when strangers came. They were used, to hunt animals that we had to eat to survive. They were our night watchman. If anything came prowling at night, the dogs would either run it off or let us know there were intruders on the place. Dogs were very important in the laid back country existence we experienced.

We also had cows. They also served three purposes. One, the cows provided us with fresh milk and butter; two, about once a year we would slaughter one for meat and food supply and three, in the fall of the year before winter came we could sell some of them for cash. We would then have money to make the winter.

We also had some hogs. You always wanted to keep at least three or four sows. Hogs had only two purposes. The first was for meat—fresh meat and salted down and smoked meat. You could use it and the meat could be traded. In the spring we would trade hog meat – trade a ham for some potatoes, or peanuts or some corn from someone else. That was one of the reasons we were so glad to go to church, so we could see who was running low on something we could trade. There was a lot of value in a trade. In fact you could trade for more, than you could by just selling and buying. Those old people knew how to trade and they still got along good.

There were those people who would have a horse and a mule. A mule you could let the women and kids use. They could do things with a mule that you wouldn't want them to do with a horse. A horse was high spirited and fast, whereas a mule was slow, mostly gentle, and unlikely to have a runaway. People valued a mule a lot more than a horse in our community for farming. But if you had to go across the bottom to the next community, you could get on your horse and just trot on over and you would be on your way back before someone on a slow mule would be arriving. Horses were not as valuable as a good heavy mule. Everyone would've like to have had a horse, but most couldn't afford both, so they had to choose the one that was most useful, that usually being a good heavy duty work mule. The women and children could use a good mule to clean out the chicken house, hang it to a slide and go to the spring: there was no worrying about anyone getting hurt by a mule running away or stepping on somebody. If you got stepped on by a mule, you had to be slow yourself. Most mules would not try to step on you and it was almost unheard of to get kicked by a mule. But with a horse, on the other hand, you had to be very careful. You could get kicked, trampled on, stepped on; sometimes old horses would just act up and have a run away.

A sorghum patch also had a triple value. First the forage would be taken, off the sorghum, by stripping off the leaves. A board would be shaped like a knife with a handle and the flat end would be like your blade. This anvil was then used to beat the leaves off the sorghum. The forage was saved and put in the shed for your cows and horses to eat later. The head of the sorghum would then be cut and that would be your chicken feed. The sorghum stalks; you would crush the juice out into a pan and cook the juice. As it went through the levels of cooking it would cook into syrup. It took an experienced person to feed the mill and cook the syrup without it burning. There was a hose connected to a long pole that went around and around to crush the stalks and one person would be taking out the old stalks and putting in new ones. It took someone with good attention to keep up with the crusher. A good sorghum patch was highly valuable. It provided feed for the animals and syrup for the family.

Another use for a mule was to hook to a slide. They needed an animal that was slow and sure footed. That's why the mule was so useful. They would go out into the woods and pick up pine knots, old pine trees when they died and fell. The center, known as the heart, it would then be picked up and put on the slide. You would use this wood for cooking the syrup.

"DETERMINATION"

No Formal Education, but Great Determination

THERE WAS A man when I was young who could not read or write, but he was a timber buyer. This man could cruise timber without the ability to count. You've heard the term box car letters, well you could use letters that size and he would not know his name. But this man could cruise timber and come out knowing how much was there. What he did, he would use pea gravels. He would have a sock in his back pocket with pea gravels inside and he would pour some of the rocks and put them in his right hand and then into his right front pocket. He could buy standing timber or he could buy timber already cut. Each time he estimated a load of standing timber he would shift one rock from his right front pocket to his left front pocket. He could buy standing timber. He could stand and look at a grove of timber and he would shift a rock to his left front pocket. When he bought cut timber and he saw a load, he would shift the rock from his right front pocket to his left rear pocket. When he got home to his wife, he would take the rocks out of his left front pocket and his wife and daughter would count the rocks and then his wife could figure how much money he owed the people for the timber. She could count the money and put it in a bank bag. Back then the banks would give you a bag as a courtesy, a little green bag with drawstrings with two little black balls. She would put the money in the bag and he would pay the people for the timber. He would always use the term, "Let's go in the house and get on the table and count this money and make sure its right". He couldn't count any more than 1, 2, 3, so when he went out into the woods and there was wood already cut, in those days a lot of people owned a sizable tracts of land and in the spring they would actually cut and stack the wood. They would do what you called penning pulp wood. They would take a square pen; it took eight pens of wood to make a load. Every time he would see a pen of wood he would shift a rock from his right front pocket to his left front pocket. He would stand and say, "Oh, I see 1, 2, 3, oh you got a lot of it". He would then go into the procedure of shifting rocks. This man was so good at that until other men would come and use him to cruise timber for them and pay him $8 or $10. In those days, $8 or $10 was good money for a half days work.

The roads would get bad in the winter and he would leave his truck up beside the highway because he didn't want to drive down into the community and tear up the roads. But those were the good old days when you could leave your vehicle and everyone in the community knew who's vehicle it was. The worst thing that could happen would be someone would run out of gas and get a couple gallons out of your tank. But usually they would come to you the next week and say "Hey look, I borrowed a couple of gallons of gas out of your truck. Here is a $1 that will probably pay for the gas. I know I got two gallons because I have a two gallon can".

If this man could make it back then with his literacy handicap and he didn't die a poor man – I'm not saying he was rich, but he did have a comfortable living. I have a problem with people today just giving up and becoming dependent on others. So when you take a look at the opportunities of today and there are so many, the opportunities are much greater than the opportunities were back then. So if you want success, just ask yourself, how bad do you want it? For the opportunities are there and they are just waiting for someone to take advantage of them. There is no need for robbing, stealing, killing and taking anything that you didn't work for.

Across the bottoms, there was a man in another community. He was so uneducated until he was smart. He raised goats and pigs. He invented his own language. You'd go over to his place and tell him you wanted to buy a couple of goats. He would tell you to "Come back tomorrow, I'll have some up in the pen, I'll have them in the pen for you to pick from". In those days people who lived in the country let their animals run free because the animals would come home every evening. They would give them a little feed, which would make them come home every day. This man invented him a language for numbers. He would count like this, 1, 2, this one, that one, and another one and that was five. Until you did business with him a few times, you never knew what he was doing. He literally did not know his numbers past 2 so he would fill in with words for the other numbers. If he had to count to ten, he would repeat the process, 1, 2, this one, that one, another one. This was done with both hands which meant 10. One hand was five. If he had to count to fifteen he would go, 1, 2, this one, that one and another one. That way two hands and a tail meant 15. His wife understood exactly what he was talking about. People used to have a big barbeque to get people back together. People went to church, but because of work and other things they would slack up and the preacher would have this gathering to get everyone back interested in church. So he would feed them. Someone would go across the bottoms and go to this guy and get 2 or 3 goats from him. He wasn't the only one to sell goats, but a lot of people used him. Usually if it was going to be a big barbeque, they would get three goats and a pig. You would take the horse and a slide. There was a road that went over there, but you couldn't drive a car because you had to cross the creek. On the creek there was a forting place which meant the banks of the creek went down sloping. The creek was not that deep and it had a gravel bottom. You could cross it easily with a horse and a slide. If you got a pig, you would tie all four feet and put him on the slide, but if you got a goat, you'd take the end of the rope and make a lasso, put the goat in it, move up another hitch and make another lasso until you got all the goats on one rope. If you were riding a horse, it would make you sore at first, because the goats usually wouldn't act right and kept pulling back. After a mile or so they would get tired of pulling back and they all would line up and go with you.   This guy was an amazing fellow. He never had very much, but he and his wife and children were always happy and seemed like they were glad to see people. He was glad to do business with somebody.

Each time I talk about my dad I talk about us sitting in the room by the heater and I talk about my mother reading the bible at night, sitting by the heater. In those days, when I was a boy, we only had one heater in the whole house. The rest of the house would be cold. We would have a heater in the living room and everyone in the winter would sit in this one room. The bedrooms were not heated. The kitchen was only heated by the stove. In fact, I can remember going in the kitchen early in the morning and breaking ice on the water to get a drink. I talk about sitting by the heater because that was basically what we did in the wintertime. I remember my dad sitting by the heater and talking to us boys. He would say, "Boys, you can't sell apples off an empty wagon. You need to go to school and get an education. You can't sell apples off an empty wagon. You need to know how to do something. High school is for everyone, college may not be for everyone, but then go to trade school. You need some education, because you can't sell apples off an empty wagon."

The company I work for, I notice a lot of times when there is one high tech welding job that they need done, they will send clear across the county for a welder, a particular welder, and this guy is good. Out of 15 or 20 welds, he might have to ground one after its x-rayed. He is a small stature man, real easy to get alone with. He doesn't brag very much, but I did hear him say one time that he could weld up any crack he could step across. I guess you could call that bragging, but I can truthfully say he has earned the right. The thing that is so remarkable is that when they x-ray his welds, they are only looking at his work. I have yet to see them look at an x-ray and be concerned about the color of the skin of the welder, that's no big deal. Out of all the years this man has been coming out there working for the company, when they x-ray his welds they always turn out good. The kind of things I see now makes me feel good, because I know that my grandchildren, nieces and nephews have an opportunity. If they have to take up a collection to bury them, it won't be because society held them back. It will be because they failed to apply themselves. Because I know now that they have an opportunity. My father told me many times about when he was a young man with young children, he moved off of a man's farm to an area where his kids could go to school. Living on this man's place, he knew this man was going to want his children to work instead of going to school. So he moved, bought a 22 acre cutoff, a piece of property that was cutoff from the main piece of property by a creek. He and my mother moved onto this property, cleared it, and built a small house. He was so poor until he used pine poles for the rafters. He was determined he was going to give his kids an education so he worked that winter and got the little house built. They cleared the land and started raising a crop. The first year the land was so stumpy he couldn't plow it; he had to dig it up with a shovel. But he and my mother, in spite of the hardships raised a crop. I often heard him tell how he planted around the stumps until they finally rotted away and he removed the roots until he was able to plow. Each year he looked forward to doing better because he would have more land cleared, more roots would be out of the ground and he would be able to cultivate this land better each year. He was determined that he was going to give his children a chance at an education, and he did.

I remember the first time I got stopped by a Black state trooper. I had been to town in my old truck. As I was coming back, I came around this curve and I met him. He turned the light on, turned around and stopped me. I pulled over, sat there in my truck looking at my side view mirror and there was this black man coming up out of that car. He had to be 6'8". He finally got all the way out of the car, reached back and got his Smoky Bear hat and put it on, and asked me for my license and insurance papers. I was so proud to see that man. He probably thought I was afraid he was going to give me a ticket. Well in a way I was, but I was very cooperative. He didn't write me a real ticket, he wrote me a warning ticket – 62 in a 55. He told me to slow myself down and go on about my business, but I was so proud to see a Black state trooper that if he would have written me a ticket I would have signed the ticket with pride. I was so proud to see a Black man as a state trooper. We went from being pushed around by the law to now a lot of us are representing the law. It was in that same town a policeman pulled me over earlier. He talked to me so bad until the white man I was riding with, got upset. Now in that same town they have a Black sheriff, a Black mayor and a Black school superintendent.

On a lot of these construction jobs you see Black men walking around with note pads and making major decisions. When I was a boy that was something unheard of, it just wouldn't be tolerated. You drive through town now and see a sign saying "Slow – men working", a lot of the guys are working for the city, and they have one or two men working and about six men watching. Well slow down and have a real good look, one or two of those six men watching will be black. That's another thing that was unheard of in the old days.

At the bank now -- in the old days you might get a job sweeping or polishing the brass around the bank, be careful now you will see Black tellers and Black managers. Drive by the fire station and you will see one or two Black guys sitting out there. The opportunities are all over the place. So I tell you again, you can't sell apples off an empty wagon. You've got to go to school and get an education. There is somebody out there who wants to buy your apples. You better not mess around and break the law and end up in the courtroom. Hear Ye! Hear Ye! That guy, when they say stands for the judge, there is a good chance he might be a Black man. We have one of them in our hometown also. Opportunities are here! Arkansas – The Land of Opportunity. God Bless America.

The End!

ABOUT THE AUTHOR

MCARTHUR BILLING, known to most as Mack, was the 8th child of 12 children born to Grady and Elburdie Billing. Mr. Billing was born and reared in Union County, Arkansas, a few miles outside of a little town called Strong. He has lived a very interesting life growing up in the rural South. Many of these experiences he shares in this book. It was this rich heritage and humble surroundings that gave Mr. Billing, so much drive and determination to survive and succeed in the hostile and segregated South of the 1940's, 50's, and 60's.

The first- hand experiences he shares in this book are priceless, but his ability to rise above the bigotry, to enjoy life in a more equal opportunity South is monumental.